Financial Management for Small Business

Edward N. Rausch

amacom

A Division of American Management Associations

For Eloise,
who has made it all worthwhile

Library of Congress Cataloging in Publication Data

Rausch, Edward N.
    Financial management for small business.

    Bibliography: p.

    Includes index.
    1. Small business—Finance.   I.   Amacom.
II.   Title.
HG3726.R38   658.1'5904   78-24594
ISBN 0-8144-5499-2
ISBN 0-8144-7585-X pbk

First AMACOM paperback edition 1982.

Contents

Introduction

IF you own or operate a small business (let's say with fewer than 50 employees, or with annual sales of $500,000 or less), then your company is a member of the largest business sector in the country. The federal Small Business Administration estimates that there are about six million firms like yours scattered across the 50 states.

It's an unfortunate fact that the life of your small business stands a good chance of being a short one. According to surveys issued recently by Dun & Bradstreet, Inc., the statistical probability that you will still be in business three years from now is about one in three; for ten years your chances are less than one in eight! If those statistics shock you, you're not alone; most owners and managers don't realize what a precarious position they're in. However, you shouldn't be too worried about going out of business, for you've already taken the first step to increase the odds on the survival of your organization: you were interested enough to begin reading this book. If you go on to finish this book and then try to apply the financial principles you've learned, you will become a better manager and your business prospects will improve.

But it will take some effort on your part. You will need to

study this book, not just skim through it. Then you will have to introduce what you've learned to the people in your organization who work with financial records and who can supply the information you need. Finally, you must follow up to ensure that the financial data are both timely and complete when reported to you. Guided by some of the reports which this book outlines, you will be able to develop a plan to achieve more profitable operations, and then steer your business more confidently in the direction of that goal.

Each section of this book is as self-contained as possible. In other words, the material in each section for the most part stands alone, seldom referring to material explained elsewhere. Therefore, you can begin reading and learning where it best suits your purpose. For example, if your business is in the start-up stage or if you are thinking about expanding an existing business, start with Section I and Section II. If your business is well established but its growth has leveled out, begin with Section III—you may be able to stimulate more expansion. If the business seems to need more working capital to ensure smooth day-to-day operation, you should read Section II first—it tells you where to look for that "money tree." And no one should neglect Section IV; the best time to start planning your estate is right now!

A word of encouragement before you start. Being a financial manager is *not* a full-time job. It won't take you away for very long from the other business concerns and responsibilities that normally fill your day if you learn to apply the concept called "management by exception," wherein you exercise financial control *only at critical times, and in specific areas.*

The technique is similar to the way a commercial pilot uses all the gauges and dials on the instrument panel of an airplane. When the airplane is in flight, thousands of minor events are constantly occurring and are continually being reflected by the little pointers or signal lights located in front of the pilot. However, the pilot cannot look at all of the gauges all of the time. At certain stages of the flight, specific instruments tell him vital information; later, others command his attention. In an emergency, a warning bell or flashing light may call attention to an especially dangerous situation.

You can adopt this same principle in conducting your business affairs. Doing this, however, requires that the various financial data be *segregated*, so that each signifies only a few things. Depending upon the kind of business you operate, a variety of specialized reports should be developed. Corrective action must be targeted carefully, and there should be no doubt about the direction such action must take. By selectively reviewing your reports and by reacting only to the most pertinent data, you can "pilot" your business away from danger and along the course indicated by your profit plan.

Here are just a few examples of "exception" data that might warrant financial managerial action in different types of small businesses:

- Extreme shifts in raw material prices.
- Expansion or contraction of available cash reserves.
- Shift in volume of sales orders from one type of service to another.
- Major cost reductions, indicating a potential increase in profitability.
- Delay in collection of a significant number of receivables.
- Unexpected downtime of vital equipment.
- Undue accumulation of obsolete inventory.
- Major deviations from forecasted sales.
- Failure to meet a substantial number of delivery promises.
- An unanticipated increase in direct labor costs.

When "managing by exception," the trick is to know (1) what information you will need in order to avoid future trouble or gain an unusual advantage, and (2) how to get that information presented in the clearest, timeliest way. We hope that this book will help you in both respects.

SECTION I

Your Profit Plan
for Start-up or Growth

1

Organizing
Your Business
to Promote
Your Financial Plan

WE all plan. Every responsible adult plans his or her weekly, daily, and hourly activities and then attempts to carry out those plans. You did it this morning when you got up, dressed, and went to work. Likewise, your business needs to be planned financially if it is to function effectively. Furthermore, this financial plan must include all possible fiscal considerations, not just a simple, loosely structured goal. In other words, your business financial planning cannot be hit or miss; it must be comprehensive.

One of the more important aspects of financial planning is the organization of your firm. When considering what you want to do, it is important to think about the way in which the company is or should be set up. The functions that a business performs are affected by its organization; efficiency, too, is greatly influenced. This is true no matter how popular your product or service may be, no matter how great your financial resources are.

The Importance of Personnel in Your Plan

Let us acknowledge from the beginning that each individual's talent—yours and that of all the other personnel—is very important to your business. The success of every venture a firm undertakes rests upon the abilities and attitudes of its employees. Of course, work can be done more efficiently and therefore more profitably if the various tasks are properly arranged and assigned. The difficulty lies in selecting an organization plan that achieves the greatest profitability.

There is, in fact, no one best way to organize a small business. What may be right for your competitor down the street might be bad for you. And the reason may have nothing to do with differences in size or the nature of the commodity or service provided, but with variations in personnel. There are broad ranges of experience, skill, and motivation among the people who work for you. Naturally, this also means that as employees change by growing or learning, or by leaving the company, the organization should also change.

As long as the business is small, it is not a good idea to designate responsibilities too precisely. Such titles as "paymaster" or "sales manager" or "director of personnel" imply a rigid organizational framework and limited responsibilities. Because most of your key employees probably must be flexible in their assignments, they should be given relatively general job designations, such as "supervisor" or "foreman." This is more in keeping with the idea of a flexible organization plan.

The principal goal you should seek is *efficiency*. If the goods or services of the business are being produced on time and at an acceptable cost, then you probably have a good organization right now. When your customers change their needs or wishes, or when the qualifications and abilities of your workforce change, then the organization—especially its work assignments—should also be changed. It's as simple as that—keep the assigned work consistent with your day-to-day business requirements, and your future organizational problems will be minimal. The impact of these work assignments on profitability is discussed in Chapter 12.

Many small businesses have one prime advantage over larger competitors—that of greater output per person. Employees of your business can achieve such productivity. Proper assignment of work is half the battle; the other half depends on the way you operate the business and your personal approach to leadership. Table 1 illustrates several different managerial styles and the way in which typical employees react to them.

The table makes it apparent that the nature of your manager/employee relationships can produce a wide range of results. Bear in mind that a small business must rely on relatively few employees for its success. Frequently only one person can carry out a certain vital job, and sometimes a single individual performs several functions. Thus failure of any employee to work efficiently can be critical. Clearly, you must try to reach a balance between the practical needs of your business and the felt needs of individual workers.

This in turn suggests the importance of "human" leadership for your business, where employees are valued as people rather than as objects or commodities. To accomplish this, your approach to leadership should develop or stress the following:

- A humanistic attitude toward your employees based on their complex and shifting personal goals.
- A broad concept of your managerial power, relying on reason and collaboration (not coercion or threats) to achieve results.

- A participatory approach to your organizational objectives, replacing an inhuman or bureaucratic system.

Such leadership may not be easy for you to exercise, and it may take time to perfect. However, it can pay real dividends

Table 1. Managerial leadership styles and managerial decision sharing

Manager's Style of Leadership	Subordinate's Perception of the Business Power Source	Subordinate's View of Manager's Communication Method
Autocratic	Power held by the manager.	An order-giver who seldom explains or asks for opinion of others.
Authoritarian	Power within the responsibility of the position.	Highly directive. May apologize for "one-way" decisions but will not reverse.
Bureaucratic	Power within the rules and procedures of the system.	Dependent upon regimented and preestablished steps. Will explain but avoids deviations.
Democratic	Power within the majority of the group.	Seeks subordinate reactions. Discusses other opinions. May let subordinates share in decision making.
Participatory	Power jointly exercised by the leader and the group.	Subordinates encouraged to share in problem solving and decision making. May be viewed as leader's abdication of power.
Abdication	Power within the formal organization but outside the manager.	Random communication, mostly confined to emergency situations.

to your business, as the employees will repay a participatory attitude on your part with a greater sense of devotion and better results. Keep in mind that it is easier for the workers to feel loyal to an individual man or woman—that is, you—than to an impersonal organization (such as one of your larger competitors).

Four of the Most Common Legal Organization Forms

Regardless of the way in which you attempt to encourage personal commitment from each of your employees, you must also give consideration to the company's legal structure. Fortunately, in this case it is relatively easy to decide upon the best approach. If the business is now under way, you have already made a choice, and it is probably one of the four most popular types: proprietorship, partnership, corporation, or "Subchapter S" corporation. However, you might be better off switching structures. Therefore, this discussion will stress each of their advantages and disadvantages as though your business were still in the start-up stage.

Let's say you have inherited a few thousand dollars and you propose to use the money to start your own construction business. Should you organize as the sole proprietor, go into partnership with your best friend, or form a closely held corporation with members of your family owning the stock?

This is the same kind of question that concerns anyone who is about to start a new business venture. To answer the question meaningfully requires an understanding of the merits and limitations of each of these business arrangements.

Proprietorship

This setup can be begun or ended most easily and is also the most flexible. It simply involves *you* forming *your* company and beginning to transact business almost immediately. In other words, a proprietorship is an extension of a person, of the man or woman who heads it. There is no government approval involved. The owner is merely taxed on the business profits, which are considered part of his or her income. The owner is also personally liable for the debts of the business. When the owner dies or retires, the life of the business ends unless he or she has sold or otherwise disposed of it before that time.

Partnership

This arrangement is similar to a sole proprietorship, except that at least two people are involved. It is the easiest way for two or more individuals to set up a business. Again, no government approval is involved, the partners are each taxed personally for their business profits, and (except for certain "limited partner" relationships) are also each personally liable for the business debts or other obligations. If one partner wants to retire (or dies), the remaining partner(s) can acquire the other's interest through purchase.

Corporation

Forming a corporation usually means that you must work with a lawyer in order to draw up the articles of incorporation. It also involves filing an application with the state where you live. Every state has its own laws specifically regulating all corporations that are headquartered within its boundaries. Thus, in this country there are fifty different definitions of a corporation.

This is by far the most complex of the four organization types discussed here. Once a corporation is formed, it is considered an individual legal entity, meaning that the business has a separate existence from that of its owners. Although a corporation has a continuous legal life, the scope of activity allowed the company is restricted to those provisions specified by its charter.

The profit earned by a corporation is taxed separately from the income of its owners; it is also separately liable for its own debts. The latter fact is one of the chief merits of the corporate organization form, but the separate income tax paid on corporate profits creates double taxation for the stockholders, who are also taxed for profits paid out as dividends.

Since a corporation has an unlimited life of its own, its existence is not necessarily affected by the death or retirement of a shareholder. His or her shares of stock may be retained by the heirs, sold to someone else, or bought back by the corporation itself.

Subchapter S Corporations

This form differs from the normal corporation in several respects. In most cases, a Subchapter S structure is selected during the early life of a corporation, when losses rather than profits are anticipated. The differences between a regular corporation and the Subchapter S variety pertain entirely to federal taxes and other federal control measures. (State regulations are not involved.) The "negative" income tax that results from a yearly loss is not retained at the corporate level but may be passed to the owners of the Subchapter S corporation. Thus, they are able to write off that loss against other personal income and enjoy an overall reduction in their personal tax liability. In short, a Subchapter S corporation is a federal tax shelter for its stockholders.

Some of the important ways a Subchapter S firm differs from a regular corporation are as follows:

- A Subchapter S corporation must be organized as a "domestic" corporation, that is, chartered for domestic operations by one of the fifty states.
- The Subchapter S designation must be specifically approved each year by the board of directors of the corporation. If it should be terminated (either intentionally or by failure to act on the part of the board of directors), it cannot be reestablished for five years.
- A Subchapter S corporation must be owned by no more than ten individual stockholders, and can issue only one

"class" of common stock. Obviously, then, the Subchapter S form has been intentionally limited to a very small company.

Selecting the Legal Structure That Is Best for You

Knowing a little about each of these four business setups, you should now be in a better position to decide among them. However, regardless of how much you know, it would still be wise to consult an attorney before acting, for if you make the wrong choice, it can cost you considerable inconvenience and expense to convert later on. If you're already in business and want to switch to a different form of organization, be sure that you make a satisfactory selection this time. Here, an attorney can be especially useful.

However, no matter what advice you get, the final decision will always be yours. The remainder of this chapter offers some guidelines to keep in mind when making your selection.

Your Tax Considerations

Probably the most important planning factor concerns your taxes. No matter how well you manage your enterprise, if your taxes cannot be kept to a minimum, you may as well not be in business. Unless you can keep most of the profit you earn, why bother? However, we will not attempt to delve deeply into tax matters here—the subject is too complex, and your business situation is probably too unique for any general remarks to be useful. But at the same time, there are some basic facts you should weigh when selecting a legal status:

• Under a proprietorship or partnership, losses from the business can be written off against any other personal income, and thus can lower your overall tax liability.

• On the other hand, all the profits you earn if your business is formed as a partnership or proprietorship will be taxed by the federal government at personal income rates.

This can result in a considerably heavier tax burden than if you were taxed as a stockholder, even the major stockholder.

• Corporations pay lower income taxes, but, as previously explained, their owners are subject to a virtual double taxation as far as profit distributed by the business is concerned. Taxes are levied first at the corporate level and again when the after-tax profits are paid out as dividends to the shareholders. Note, however, that this does not apply to corporations organized under Subchapter S. For tax purposes owners of a Subchapter S corporation are treated in a manner similar to proprietors or partners.

• Restrictions on tax-deductible fringe benefits (primarily retirement provisions) are more severe under a proprietorship or partnership than under a corporation.

Formation Procedures and Costs

As indicated above, a proprietorship is easiest to start. The first step is to determine what kind of local license you must buy, if any, and to become familiar with the state taxes and fees you will be charged. Once that step is passed, you are in business.

A partnership requires only one more act—that of establishing a partnership agreement. Such an agreement may be either written or verbal, although a written agreement is strongly recommended, so that all important details can be established permanently.

"Limited" partnerships are slightly more complicated during the inception stage. Here, the partners must prepare a written agreement specifically limiting the liability of one or more of them to a given amount (no less than the amount of their investment in the partnership). At the same time, at least one member of the partnership must be designated in writing as a "general partner" in order to take on unlimited liability responsibility for the partnership in total. The written partnership agreement must then be filed with the proper official in your state. Close attention to these prescribed legal steps is necessary, otherwise all "limited" partners will revert to a "general" status and the entire procedure of liability limitation will be void.

Forming a corporation is both the most cumbersome and the most costly approach. You must conform strictly to the laws of your particular state, and you must also pay a fairly substantial charge for the privilege of incorporating. Since the various state regulations are dissimilar, only a few general requirements can be cited for your guidance. These are as follows:

- The corporation's directors must be formally selected by an election procedure and must be designated in writing.
- Formal "Articles of Incorporation" must be prepared and filed in writing with the proper state official.
- An initial incorporation tax and filing fee must be paid at the time of filing.
- An opening "official" meeting of the directors must be held to establish the identity of all organization officers and the company's method of operation (such as the payment of dividends, the time and place of meetings, the salaries and duties of the officers, and so on).

The Degree of Risk

The amount of risk that you (and any other owners of your business) will assume should be a very important item among your considerations. Your creditors will always have a prior claim on the assets of your company in the event that your debts to them cannot be settled in any other way. Thus, you may be virtually certain that your equity (or investment) in the company cannot be fully recovered if the business fails. In fact, if the business assets are not sufficient to satisfy creditor claims, you (and the other owners) may be personally liable for the difference. This personal liability can be limited or unlimited, depending upon the type of organization you have formed.

We have already indicated that the corporate structure automatically provides a real benefit—limiting the liability of its owners. Thus, incorporating limits the risk that the owners must face. On the other hand, owners of proprietorships or partnerships have completely unlimited liability. The only way to avoid this is to be a "limited" partner. (See the preceding discussion on formation procedures for an explanation.)

Will Your Business Be Easy to Administer?

A proprietorship usually provides the greatest concentration of administrative responsibility and authority. At first glance, such centralization of control would appear to be a prime advantage. However, the question of competency must be kept in mind: will you, as proprietor, be qualified to handle all the management functions alone? Even if the actual responsibility for some duties is delegated to other employees, you as the owner will have to oversee their activities and pay the penalties (or reap the rewards) for what they do. Vesting sole power and accountability in the person of the proprietor is in keeping with the concept of the proprietorship, and can be good or bad, depending on the proprietor's ability to manage.

In the case of a partnership, each partner usually shoulders part of the administrative role. Typically, the duties and responsibilities are divided fairly evenly in "general" partnerships. ("Limited" partners may be involved only partially or not at all in day-to-day management.) This ability to utilize the combined experience and knowledge of several people gives a partnership an important advantage over a sole proprietorship—as long as the partners do not disagree on policy matters. That can lead to impasses unless one of the partners is formally designated the "senior" member of the firm, with one of his responsibilities being to render final judgment regarding all disputes.

Corporations must have a board of directors, who may or may not be active in establishing policy or running the business. Generally, in a corporation the officers carry out all such functions, and as a result, a corporation is better able to avoid any inefficiency stemming from the limited ability or knowledge of the owner group. On the other hand, some of the owners, even those who own only a few shares, can become very dissatisfied with the way the corporation is being run. This is always a possibility, especially if those who are in daily control have little or no financial interest as stockholders of the corporation. Distribution of net profit is often a sore point. Owners tend to want most of the profit to be distributed; nonowner officers usually prefer to retain as much profit as possible in order to foster growth.

Potential Life Span of Your Business

When you select the legal structure for your business, you may be predetermining its longevity, that is, whether or not it will continue to operate after you retire or die. This is a most important consideration and one which is often overlooked. Generally, small business owners do not pay enough attention to problems likely to be encountered when they want to retire or when their estates are being set up. The matter is discussed more fully in Section IV. It is enough to say at this point that proprietorships and partnerships are much more perishable than corporations. Also, stock certificates, which represent a share of corporate ownership, can be sold or traded without interfering with normal operation of the corporation. This is not the case in a proprietorship or partnership, where the sale of all or any of the ownership will almost certainly create disruption.

To summarize, the longevity of a proprietorship or partnership is usually tied to the career length of the owner(s), whereas a corporation can go on virtually forever.

The Possibility of Attracting Outside Financing for Your Business

This factor will probably be more important in the long run than in your immediate business future. Although you may not believe it at the beginning, if your company is to become as successful as you want it to be, the time will come when you will need more financing. Almost every business encounters such a problem at least once. (The special difficulties in getting your hands on more money are covered in Section II; you may want to postpone a study of it at present.) The type of legal arrangement you select is significant in this respect, because of the impact of different state laws on probable sources and amounts of financing.

A proprietorship is such a well-established form of business that both its legal rights and its relationships to agents or creditors are completely clear. Under the United States Constitution, a proprietorship headquartered in one state can conduct business in all the other states without being subject to any more taxes or restrictions than are imposed on truly local businesses. This makes outside financing comparatively easy to attract from a legal standpoint. There are no state regulatory bodies; there are no fees or taxes imposed on "foreign" proprietorships. If a loan or investment is sought, it can be a confidential transaction, with the details known only to the parties involved.

A partnership is virtually the same as a proprietorship from the standpoint of freedom from state regulation. The only difference pertains to "limited" partnerships, which are more closely regulated in some states than in others. Thus, partnerships also qualify readily for additional outside financing.

In contrast, a corporation chartered under the laws of any state is a legal entity unique to that state. No other state is required to recognize "foreign" corporations (those chartered by another state), although all states do extend this recognition as a matter of custom. Nonetheless, out-of-state corporations are generally forced to comply with special regulations such as filing various legal documents, paying special taxes or other fees, and even appointing a representative within the state to act as an agent. Furthermore, since any negotiations seeking additional financing have to be carried out with the state regulatory body acting as an interested observer, special financial deals or private transactions are much more difficult for corporations to arrange than for proprietorships or partnerships. The net effect of all this is that in some states outside financing is somewhat less easy to obtain for a corporation.

Special Considerations in Organizing a Family-Owned Business

Anyone who is interested in the operation of a small business cannot dodge two basic facts of small business life: first, it is easier to run a successful business with a management team than for one person to try it alone; second, perhaps the most common way to start up a small business is to seek money within the family circle, and this often means borrowing from relatives and taking several of them into the company to help run it.

These two factors, taken together, have been largely responsible for the substantial number of family-owned small businesses operating in the United States. Yours may be one of them. If so, you are probably well aware of some of the following drawbacks of conducting your business with your relatives:

- You may be stuck with an incompetent employee whom you are reluctant to discharge because of his or her family connections.
- Differences of opinion or family feuds can carry over into the business. Conversely, serious disagreements can occur within the family over major business expenditures or such things as distribution of profits. These differences can eventually disrupt your day-to-day control of the business.
- If you die unexpectedly or simply decide to retire, your relatives will probably become deeply involved with selecting your successor, and this could adversely affect the interests of your immediate family. (Section IV addresses the many problems involved in the disposition of your business.)

It is not intended to suggest here that a family-type business cannot succeed, nor are we so impractical as to say that you should reorganize if your business is family-owned. Instead, two items of advice are offered for your consideration and possible adoption. First, be sure that all of your decisions are based solely on available facts or your own reasonable estimates. Of course, that is the only sensible rule for *any* business to follow, and the idea is hardly an original one. However, some small business owners often seek the advice of the relatives who backed them financially, and this is a certain invitation to trouble. Since it is your business, you must remain in charge. If the family begins to participate in your decision making, there will be no end to the times when they will expect, or demand, to be drawn in. It is a sure way to lose control of your company.

Second, all important rules and regulations for your business should be expressed *in writing*. Spelling out on paper what is to be done will provide you with two important benefits: (1) you will derive the usual advantages of consistency and permanency, and (2) in case of a family disagreement, the rule is available for everyone to see. If a change must be made to reconcile important differences of opinion, be sure that the compromise is also committed to paper. Written regulations tend to be perceived as "the bible" and can obviate or more easily settle family quarrels.

Conclusion

This chapter has introduced some of the important organizational questions that confront a small business operator. Although these matters are not strictly financial in nature, they are vital in providing a sound base for good financial management.

Bear in mind that the "fabric" of your organization should not interfere with conducting business or fulfilling your financial plan. Unfortunately, there is no such thing as an "ideal" business organization; at best, there are only recommended approaches toward that elusive goal. Once you properly appreciate business organization, you will be on your way toward that most satisfying of all goals—being in business for yourself and making good money at it.

2

Budgeting
Your Financial Plan

ONE of the most important things you should do in developing a financial plan for your business is to decide how much money you want to make and when you want to make it. Do you want to end up a millionaire or just be able to feed your family? It may sound unrealistic, but in order to plan financially you will need to set up a practical long-range goal. That goal should also be related to your current income and to whatever money or property you have been able to accumulate up to now.

The first step is to set an objective for next year's income. In plain terms, how much do you think your efforts should be worth next year? (Remember that you ought to receive a return for the time spent operating your business *and* a return on the dollar investment you have made.) In trying to decide what your yearly contribution to the business is worth, you should sharpen the focus of your long-range "wealth target";

that will be the first step toward establishing an annual budget for your business.

These remarks may raise another basic question for you—why budget in the first place? Your business may still be in the start-up stage, with enough other problems to worry about. Why take on another headache? Many small businesses never prepare a budget, and they don't all fail. Perhaps yours has been operating for a while with reasonable success without a budget. Why start one now? What will you get in return for the extra work?

The best way to answer the question "Why budget?" is to show what a budget really is and also what it isn't. Contrary to what you may have thought, a budget isn't simply another set of accounting records. In fact, budgeting does not even represent an accounting function. It is a financial management function, with special emphasis on the word management. Of course, your accountant (or bookkeeper) will have to keep score for you by helping you calculate the budgetary figures and then by comparing them with operating results. But that is needed simply to give you an information base. Armed with this information, you can first *analyze;* then *interpret;* and finally *react*. Essentially, then, a budget is not an accounting activity but a management tool. If you decide not to budget, you are giving up a valuable measure of administrative control over your business.

The Benefits of Budgeting

Let us consider all of the things a budget does, and how it can help you do a better managing job and make more money.

One of the most significant advantages your business can derive from budgetary forecasting is that the very process requires constant awareness of problems and possibilities. You may never take the time to think about such matters consistently unless you adopt the budget philosophy. It is a common human tendency to put off difficult decisions.

Perhaps you could be pardoned for avoiding perplexing financial considerations in view of the many other demands upon your time. However, all too often a sudden financial crisis will arise forcing you to solve a money problem by "shooting from the hip." In contrast, when you begin to develop formal financial plans for the future, and when the system makes it necessary to study deviations from these plans, you will become a much better manager. Your financial administration will be more consistent, and there will undoubtedly be fewer unexpected emergencies in the first place.

Another important benefit of budgeting is that every segment of your business will become involved. Each supervisor within your company who is responsible for either income or expenses will have to help you develop the budget. The result will be a consolidation of the thinking of key personnel as well as your own. Since budgeting will require their participation, the supervisory employees are more likely to be "sold" on the budget and therefore more willing to abide by the end result.

A final general benefit of budgeting is that it gives you a way to formally express your financial policies. After you have completed a budget for the year and distributed copies to the responsible employees, they'll be better able to understand your intentions for that period. If you intend to cut back, your budget will indicate how much and where. If you plan to expand, the budget will clearly show your increased income and expense targets.

Control Afforded by a Budget

As soon as your budgetary plan is prepared, you automatically possess a device for steering the business toward your goals. That is because what the business *does* can be easily measured against what it was *intended to do.* If your company runs into trouble, you can take more precise corrective action. Your budget will be broken down into different elements and one or more of those elements will contain the seed of the trouble.

In addition, when you spend in accordance with a budget,

it will be *controlled spending.* By carefully scrutinizing all pro-jected costs before approving them, you can prevent waste. Of course, you will have to follow up any cost overruns; the budget can't police itself. However, with a budget, you can easily tell what part of the business was responsible for the excess costs.

Coordination Provided by a Budget

The concept of *balance* in your business will be another automatic by-product of budgeting. By drawing supervisors from all parts of your business into the preparation of the budget, you will prevent any unit from expanding out of proportion or, equally important, from being ignored. The budget will ensure that each segment of the business makes a contribution toward earning revenue and/or is allocated operating funds in proportion to its productivity.

Also, a budget will help you keep your business in balance with the outside world. You should probably not undertake an expansion at the same time the rest of the local business community is about to "go bust." And if you do decide to go ahead, the budgetary procedure will ensure that analysis and planning are carried out carefully.

Summary of Budgetary Benefits

To summarize, here are the general benefits you can ex-pect your business to achieve from budgeting:

- A more organized and foresighted attitude toward the financial future of the organization.
- Assurance that all responsible personnel are viewing the financial objectives of the business on the same terms.
- The ability to coordinate and/or consolidate diverse ap-proaches toward earning or spending of money.
- The possibility of analyzing how successful your financial planning for the future proved to be, and of determining what, if anything, went wrong.

Budgetary Steps to Be Followed

There is, of course, more to budgeting than reading about the benefits. You must be prepared to do some extra work yourself in order to establish the budget, and also to authorize initial overtime for others in your organization who must be brought into the process.

It would be a mistake to assume that budgeting for a business can be done piecemeal or without disrupting some work routines. As you may have discovered by now, resistance always follows change, unless there has been advance preparation. This means that the first step in budgeting is to convey the idea to your key staff. There may be only one other supervisory employee who will take part, but there could be ten or fifteen or more; the number will depend on the size of your business and how you delegate authority. But no matter how many or how few there are, all employees who have any responsibility for making or spending money must be told three things about budgeting.

First, they must be told that you are in favor of the concept and intend to see that it is adopted. Second, they must be informed generally what will be involved on their part in preparing the advance estimates. And third, they must understand clearly that the budget is to be followed, and that their performance will be measured against the budgetary projections that they themselves had a hand in compiling. In other words, your management staff must realize that you mean business about budgeting. If they accept the yearly budget on those terms, they can be persuaded to help you develop and introduce it and, finally, to follow it.

Backing into Budgeting

The easiest budget to prepare for next year is one modeled after last year's actual performance. That is the recommended way for you to commence this program. The only case where such an approach is impractical is when your business is just getting started; then, you'll have to make the necessary projections using your best judgment.

Once a reliable set of administrative disciplines to support the budget process has been worked out and installed in your company, you may want to consider more elaborate procedures such as "project budgeting" or the currently popular "zero-based budget." But hold off. For at least the first two years you should plan ahead by first looking backward. And don't be put off by the term "backing into budgeting"; it indicates a method, not disapproval. The essential budgeting steps described below will help you understand why your approach to budgeting should be kept as simple as possible in the beginning.

Building the Foundation for Your Budget

When calculating the coming year's budget, project your best estimate of the *volume* of products or services (or both) that you expect the business to do next year and the *revenue* that will be received. Divide these estimates into monthly figures based on the amounts of your past monthly billings, then proceed as follows:

1. Start with last year's monthly revenues, broken down by product or service line.
2. Adjust for strong positive or negative trends in your revenue stream if any can be detected.
3. Increase or decrease expected revenues in accordance with your anticipated competitive position in those markets where other companies are a factor.
4. Finally, make your best guess as to the condition of the national and local economies and/or the economic cycle for your industry.

These monthly estimates of your sales or rentals represent "foundation" data on which your entire yearly budget will depend, and therefore they must be constructed very carefully. It is suggested that you take the responsibility for preparing them yourself: there is a managerial judgment function involved here that you alone are probably best equipped to perform.

As will be explained below, the remaining basic data can be calculated by your bookkeeper with directions provided by you. However, all such calculations will depend on the monthly sales or rental projections that you have developed.

Your next step should be to obtain an estimate of your monthly cost of sales or rentals, by product or service. It will probably be quite laborious for the bookkeeper to produce initial cost projections of this type "from the ground up." Therefore you might want to adopt the following equally satisfactory shortcut:

1. Ask your bookkeeper to categorize all your business expenses as either *fixed* or *variable,* or partially fixed or partially variable. (A fixed expense does not change when the business volume picks up or declines, whereas a variable expense is directly related to volume.)

2. Have your bookkeeper compute separate totals of all variable labor and material expenses for the last previous business year. If you have subdivided sales or rentals by product line, have the bookkeeper do the same for these two types of variable expenses. You now have a rough approximation of last year's total *direct* cost of sales or rentals (that is, your variable expenses), broken down by direct labor cost and direct material cost. This is far from being a detailed compilation of individual direct product or service costs, but it is good enough for budget purposes.

3. Your bookkeeper can now determine next year's direct cost percentages by product or service line. The following two formulas should be used:

$$\text{Direct labor cost \%} = \frac{\text{variable labor cost by product or service line}}{\text{estimated yearly sales (revenue)}}$$

$$\text{Direct material cost \%} = \frac{\text{variable material cost by product or service line}}{\text{estimated yearly sales (revenue)}}$$

4. The final step is to apply these percentages to the monthly estimates of sales or rentals that you have already

made for next year. This will give you the basic cost and sales figures that should be used to govern all other budgetary estimates. The following two formulas should be used:

Monthly direct labor cost = direct labor cost % × monthly revenue

Monthly direct material cost
$$= \text{direct material cost} \% \times \text{monthly revenue}$$

If you carry any "on account" sales or rentals, there is one additional step that must be taken. It is to establish the "lag" that exists between the day you record a sale or rental and the day your customer makes the payment. This information is needed to permit the business cash flow to be planned, as a part of the budgetary process.

The first thing to be done is to request the bookkeeper to calculate your accounts-receivable turnover. You may already possess a quick means of getting this information if the book-keeper customarily "ages" your individual receivables.* In such a case, only one additional analysis of the separate accounts will provide the average collection period. If not available through aging, the following two-step process will provide approximately the same information:

1. Accounts-receivable turnover = $\dfrac{\text{total yearly sales and/or rentals on account}}{\text{outstanding accounts receivable at year end}}$

2. Average collection period = $\dfrac{360 \text{ days}}{\text{accounts-receivable turnover}}$

With the resulting data, you will be able to find the answer to that all-important question: "How long must I wait to get my money?" The way to apply such information to your cash planning will be explained later in this chapter.

In order to be able to project the offsetting cash outflow

---

* Aging is the process of separating accounts receivable into groups according to the time elapsed since their payment became due. This is done for the purpose of estimating how many accounts will eventually become uncollectible and how much money will be owed on such accounts.

for your business, a similar two-step calculation must be carried out for your current accounts payable. You will then be able to determine how long, on the average, your business has been delaying payment for materials purchased on account. The pertinent formulas are:

1. Accounts-payable turnover

$$= \frac{\text{total materials, supplies, and services purchased for the year on account}}{\text{total unpaid accounts payable at year end}}$$

2. Average payment period $= \dfrac{360 \text{ days}}{\text{accounts-payable turnover}}$

By carrying out the steps involved in laying the foundation for your budget, you will have made reasonable estimates of the revenue the business can expect to achieve. You will also have learned the direct costs of doing business. Further, you can establish the projected time lag involved in receiving payment from your customers and in making payment to your creditors. These data will be well worth the time spent in preparation, because your estimates will be useful in many other ways, over and above the budgetary process. The same applies to the following two, final computation procedures required for your yearly budget.

Determining Your Anticipated Fixed Costs

Fixed business costs are sometimes also called "overhead" or "burden," the implication being that they are extra or unnecessary. If that is your belief, it is well to reflect that your own salary would most likely be included among the fixed costs of your business. (As explained earlier in this chapter, fixed costs are those that do not vary with the volume of sales or rentals.)

Since these costs do not fluctuate in proportion to sales or rental revenue, the individual expense items are much easier to estimate and control. At the same time, fixed costs are generally made up of many different kinds of cash outflow, including salaries, supplies, heat, light, depreciation, taxes, insurance, and so on. Thus, a fairly detailed analysis of last year's results is necessary to produce next year's estimates. This, in, turn, should call for participation by the supervisors in your company—those responsible for spending or approving the expenditure of money.

You may remember that the procedure outlined above for compiling your direct costs of sales or rentals also involved the calculation of a fixed cost total for the previous year. In other words, your bookkeeper should have already developed a composite of what the business spent last year for all fixed cost items. This will provide a handy goal for you. Take the bookkeeper's total and then decide whether you want to change it. (In these times, it's always a good idea to try for a reduction of 5 percent or so in your fixed-cost target for the coming year.) Simply question and adjust, reduce or eliminate individual expense items until you force the total down to approximate your goal.

Remember that this is the right time to be hard-nosed. If you want to hold future fixed costs to a minimum (and who doesn't?), then insist that the supervisors keep going over their budgetary estimates until they get down to realistic totals. These are the maximum expenses that you will tolerate during the upcoming year. Furthermore, the responsible people in your business will accept the figures because they helped set those annual totals. As soon as you have reached agreement as to the yearly amounts, your bookkeeper can easily divide each category into twelve equal parts. That's all there is to it. You will have produced a monthly fixed-cost budget.

If you take this approach, you can reduce the nagging over expenses for all of next year. When someone wants to spend a few dollars, he can simply check the appropriate fixed-cost *actual* total versus the *budget* total for the month. If any money still remains uncommitted, the expenditure should go through. In this fashion, you can spread, within limits, the authority for spending. You will also notice a sense of greater responsibility among your key staff.

Establishing Your Projected "Nonoperating" Income and Costs

Almost every company experiences income and outgo during the year that are not related to normal business transactions. These are categorized as "nonoperating" and are the result of one-of-a-kind situations. Generally, the cost incurred or the product or service dispensed is totally different from that which your business is used to. Some of these transactions are described below.

Settlement of a lawsuit stemming from an accident. The damages awarded the victim would be a nonoperating expense, assuming you were the party being sued, and a nonoperating income if you had filed the suit.

Rental receipts (unless you are in the real estate business). These would be classed as nonoperating income and might be earned by renting out surplus property owned by the business.

Payment of back taxes. Such payment would be a nonoperating expense if the tax liability was not anticipated during the period when it should have been paid.

Interest income. This would be nonoperating income if it was earned by the business from deposits of surplus funds in a savings institution.

Inventory spoilage. This would be a nonoperating expense if it was not a routine loss (for example, if it occurred as the result of a fire or flood) and was not covered by insurance.

The list of nonoperating costs and income could be extended ad infinitum, since it is impossible to predict everything that could occur regarding your business. Thus, the best way to anticipate next year's nonoperating income and expense is by "backing" into the totals, that is, by basing them on what happened last year.

How Budgeting Can Be Related to Cash Planning

Your company will have a unique cycle of cash receipts and disbursements. While all business operations are generally similar, every firm tends to have certain qualities that make it different from any other. Thus, the "cash cycle" of each business varies somewhat. A conceptual model of a cash cycle is presented in Figure 1. Study it briefly; notice the various kinds of transactions involved and their interrelationships.

If there were no fluctuations in your business volume, you could work out a standard cash-flow plan, relating what you spent to what you received. Unfortunately, your company (like any other business) probably cannot be assured of a steady flow of income throughout the year. Thus, your cash outlay must also vary from month to month.

The income and expense projections that you produce for budgeting can be made to do double duty—that is, they can help you plan the best use of available cash as well as help you prepare for future outlays. The best way to accomplish both objectives is to develop an actual cash budget. A separate budgeting of cash will require extra bookkeeping; however, the end result can be one of the most important of your financial management tools. The business may be operating successfully in all respects except for a shortage of cash; yet that one deficiency can create some very serious problems for you. There is no business weakness more significant than the inability to pay wages or to meet other obligations when due. To avoid this condition should be one of your prime concerns, and a cash budget can be the answer.

Two Kinds of Cash

It goes without saying that a satisfactory financial plan for your company is one that enables you to pay current bills. The plan should also provide money for modernization of facilities and for future business expansion. What you really need to satisfy both purposes is two kinds of cash, which are likely to come from different sources.

First, your business requires *working capital*. This is the money you normally use to cover day-to-day costs. We are speaking here of payments for your *direct* business expenses

Figure 1. A typical business cash cycle.

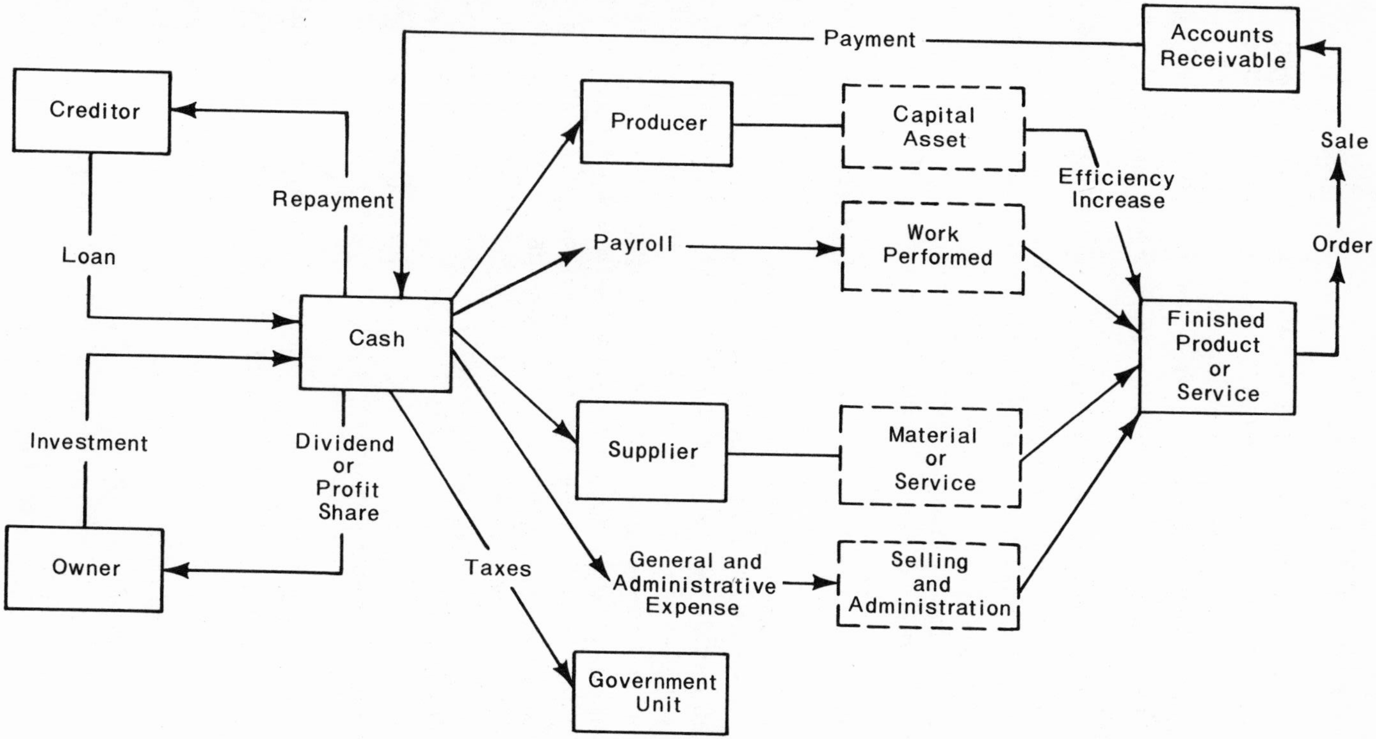

(those variable expenses which are incurred in supplying the products or services to your customers) plus *indirect* expenses (fixed costs). Second, you may occasionally need money for *capital expenditures*—additions to or replacement of your plant, office, equipment, or tools.

In most cases, your fund of working capital will be derived from regular business receipts, although you may occasionally need to supplement this by negotiating a short-term loan (repayable in one year or less). In contrast, the cash used for capital expenditures will probably come from profits earned over the years and retained in the business (instead of being distributed to the owners). If that source is insufficient, a long-term loan (repayable in from two to ten years) may be arranged. From time to time, additional equity investments in the business may also be recruited in order to raise money for capital expenditures.

Before turning our attention to the management of working capital—the area where most financial problems occur—it will be useful to discuss the best use of any cash surplus that the business may build up from time to time. This could be funds not immediately required for working capital (possibly available for as short a term as thirty days); however, it would more likely be money which has been gradually saved to pay for a sizable capital facility some time in the future. No matter where the money comes from, if it's available, you ought to use it to earn some nonoperating income. Failure to put the cash to such use results in what is called an "opportunity cost"—revenue lost when an opportunity for earnings is not taken.

In order to really appreciate the potential for income which surplus cash represents, the following few simple time–money relationships must be understood:

- The value of a certain sum of money, if invested, *grows* as time passes.
- The amount of investment needed to produce a specified future sum *decreases* as the time allowed to produce that sum *increases*.

- Both of the above effects are magnified as the available rate of return is increased.

What these relationships mean is simple: you do not need a lot of money to invest, and the longer you keep it invested, the better. If you expect to use the spare cash within a month or two, put it in a savings account or buy a short-term certificate of deposit. If you can leave it untouched for a year or more, you might want to consider municipal bonds, treasury notes, or a longer-term certificate of deposit. A banker or a broker can advise you on this. The main point to keep in mind is that your spare cash should *always* be working for you. We've said that cash used for daily business operations is "working capital"; make sure that your surplus money works, too.

How to Avoid a "Cash Crisis"

If your chief concern regarding available money has been "Do I have enough to pay the monthly bills?" or "Can I meet the next payroll?" you are probably placing too much emphasis on immediate cash needs. Not that you can ever ignore the debts which come due tomorrow, but you should also pay attention to longer-range requirements for cash. In fact, you ought to be planning your cash flow a year in advance, the same period as for your budget. Unless you look ahead far enough, a sizable and unforeseen fluctuation in volume can catch you off guard. Either too much business or too little can have the same result—a temporary but serious scarcity of working capital. Financial experts call such a condition a "cash crisis," and it is one of the most common causes of small business failure.

How can you avoid such a dangerous possibility? There's only one way—by advance planning. Planning ahead may not earn a dollar more for you, but it will tell you when major cash outflows are likely to occur. With enough advance notice you can take the steps needed to cut down on spending or to negotiate a short-term loan from your bank. In other words, you will be prepared.

Consider the projection of cash flows displayed in Figure 2, and compare the required entries with the estimates you listed as necessary for your yearly budget (subdivided into months). You will find that exactly the same kinds of projections and totals are involved. From line 1 through line 30 of Figure 2, your bookkeeper ought to have no trouble completing the entries in a few hours, assuming the annual budgetary estimating has been done.

The only processing required to complete line 31 is to subtract line 30 from line 21. And there you have it—the projected cash surplus or deficit for your business, broken down for every month of the year. Obviously the amounts will only be approximations, since every entry on this statement is based on guesswork. However, because the guesses are "educated," they will provide the best cash-flow guidance for the future that you can get.

To complete the projection of cash flows statement, your monthly cash requirements should be estimated and entered on line 32. You will then be able to determine whether a surplus or a deficit of money is likely for any given month. The latter possibility should warn you to prepare to raise extra funds. Advance negotiations with your banker would be the recommended way to do this. (Borrowing is discussed in more detail in Chapter 4.) In case loans are contemplated, lines 33 through 36 of the projection of cash flows statement provide for entry of the amount of the proposed loans as well as their repayment schedules.

Performing Budgetary and Cash "Management by Exception"

Developing a yearly budget and projecting your anticipated monthly cash flow is not the entire battle. It is also necessary to arrange "feedback of performance" information to show the extent to which the business's actual revenues and expenses deviate from what was planned. In addition, a set of contingencies should be outlined, to be followed when the performance deviations reach serious proportions. This

Figure 2. Projection of cash flows.

Year Ending

	ENTRIES	JAN	FEB	MAR	APR	MAY	JUN	JUL	AUG	SEP	OCT	NOV	DEC
PROFIT OR LOSS	1 Net Sales												
	2 Less: Materials used												
	3 Direct labor												
	4 Other manufacturing expense												
	5												
	6 Cost of Goods Sold												
	7 Gross Profit												
	8 Less: Sales expense												
	9 General and administrative expense												
	10 Equipment depreciation												
	11 Operating Profit												
	12 Less: Other expense (income)												
	13 Income tax provision												
	14												
	15 Net Profit/Loss												
CASH IN AND OUT	16 Cash Balance (opening)												
	17 Plus Receipts: Receivable collections												
	18												
	19												
	20 Nonoper. proceeds												
	21 Total												
	22 Less: Disbursements: Trade payables												
	23 Direct labor												
	24 Other M'fg expense												
	25 Sales, gen'l and adm. exp.												
	26 Fixed-asset additions												
	27 Income taxes												
	28												
	29 Dividends or withdrawals												
	30 Total												
	31 Cash Excess/Deficit												
	32 Minimum cash requirement												
	33 Proposed Loan Receipts												
	34												
	35 Proposed Loan Repayments												
	36												
	37 Planned Cash Balance												

strategy is sometimes called *financial management by exception.* To provide sufficient data for an appropriate managerial response, your financial management by exception reports should have the following general characteristics:

1. The "exception" reports should be scheduled on a regular basis (such as monthly or quarterly), but actually prepared only if there is really an emergency.

2. The "exception" reports should highlight the most significant data, which you will need when deciding how to react. For example, in the case of a follow-up procedure for receivables, a "threshold" number of past-due days should be selected as a starting point. Then, only the few accounts which exceed that threshold should be included in a "delinquent accounts receivable" report which is given to you or a subordinate responsible for collections. If there are no such accounts, the report need not and should not be issued.

3. The "exception" reports should comprise an organized "network" of information, rather than a few statements feeding isolated data to you. The delinquent-accounts-receivable data, for instance, should not be submitted alone, but together with other related reports, such as total sales report, summary of salesmen's performance, report of products sold, and so on. Not all of these reports would apply strictly to budgetary performance or cash flow; however, each would relate to all the others and all would be applicable to the selling activities of your business. Information gleaned from some of these other reports could affect your campaign to counteract an undesirable increase in past dues. For instance, the collection effort might be less strenuous during a period of sharply rising sales (as reflected by the total sales report). Under those conditions, the rise in delinquencies could be partly attributed to dealing with more customers.

4. One of the most important functions of these "exception" reports is to supply you with the earliest possible sign of trouble. This can only be done if specific data are identified as being especially important. For example, if a particular production or service process always requires use of a certain commodity, then a scarcity of that commodity or a change in

its price could affect the production or service. If a regular "inventory status report" is issued by your bookkeeper, the situation regarding the critical commodity could be flagged in some way, possibly by entering the quantity in a "critical" column. An even more useful procedure would be for your bookkeeper to attach a "critical" list to the inventory status report, thus enabling you to promptly identify the few critical items and follow up on them. The report could then be turned over to the person regularly responsible for buying production material for your company.

Financial management by exception is another case of that important principle—don't supply the boss with extraneous information, just provide enough facts to guide his or her decision. What's needed to make the "critical" list a useful early-warning device is to, first, set up the list so that the mere presence of an item indicates something unusual about the item; second, carefully describe the item by name or number; and third, in addition to indicating the on-hand quantity, monthly usage figures should show how long the stock will last.

It is not within the province of this book to describe all the possible "exception" reports that could be related to budgetary performance or to the availability of working capital. However, as owner/operator of your business, you will have to select the kinds of information that you need to keep track of. The following list shows some of the more common management concerns, and might be useful as a guide in setting up your own "exception" reports.

Sales or rental revenues off target.
Variances in product or service sales mix.
Unexpected modifications in rental patterns.
Shortfalls in attaining profitability objectives.
Equipment with excessive and costly downtime.
Abnormal cost of maintaining facilities.
Production labor-cost variances.
Production material-cost variances.
Shipping or delivery delays.

Cash in excess or short supply.
Orders not processed on schedule.
Excessive number of accounts not paid when due.
Capital spending higher than planned.
Dividends below normal.

Another crucial aspect of a budgetary management by exception system, in addition to the actual information reported, is the way in which you react when receiving a report indicating a crisis. First, your reaction must be prompt and decisive. Second, it is important that several courses of action be laid out ahead of time if at all possible. For example, referring to the delinquent-accounts-receivable data, an "all-out" collection procedure might be worked out in advance. Also, you could make prior arrangements with a bank to set up an emergency-loan program using some of your receivables as collateral. Having prepared both of these contingency plans, you will be in a strong position for that time when delinquent receivables exceed the "critical" point. Then, you simply specify that either or both contingency plans be carried out. This eliminates the need for rash action and minimizes error or delay in solving the cash-flow problems that the emergency has created.

Conclusion

The purpose of this chapter has been to explain several basic budgetary techniques which are important in a small business, thus setting the stage for other financial management processes. For example, how to acquire equity capital, the money used to start or expand a business. An owner's equity capital represents the largest fund that a typical small business will have to draw upon, and, as we have seen, the proper application of budgeting and the effective employment of equity capital is one and the same. Other uses of a good business budget will be discussed in succeeding chapters.

Throughout this discussion, considerable stress has been given your role as the owner or operator of the business in formulating a budget. Seeking the advice or help of your bookkeeper and key members of your staff has been suggested, but, in the final analysis, the responsibility must rest with you. This is as it should be, since you are, in most cases, also the chief architect of objectives and strategies for your business. If you understand how to budget for results as described herein, the budgeting will become a real help in the financial management of your business.

SECTION II

Sources of Money
to Implement
Your Profit Plan

3

Seeking Funds
to Finance
Your Profit Plan

IF you are like most small business operators, your company began its existence "strapped for cash." With most firms, this underfinanced condition continues all the way through the start-up stage and may last considerably longer than that. In fact, some small businesses never do attain a comfortable cash position. Instead, they always seem on the verge of bankruptcy.

In short, it isn't necessarily disgraceful for a small business to be underfinanced, but it does represent a definite danger to its existence. If your organization needs more financing, now is the time to begin seeking it. This chapter describes some possible sources of investment money and includes advice on how to persuade people to "fund" your profit plan. In addition, it covers some of the advantages and drawbacks that various sources of funds can represent.

Formalizing Your Proposed Profit Plan

Before considering where to look for money, it may help to refer briefly to the previous chapter on budgetary financial planning. If your quest for more cash is to be successful, you must know in advance how much is needed and what will be done with it, and those details can best be determined through the budgeting process. If anything, looking for more financing is but another good reason for adopting a budget—it will aid in explaining to a potential source of new funds just how the money will be used.

Your budget will serve as the backbone of the formal financial proposal that should be put together whenever additional money is sought. Depending upon how much you want and where you intend to look, this proposal can be either elaborate or of more modest proportions. For instance, if you are trying to attract a professional investor—typically a wary individual with thousands of dollars to work with—your proposal must be polished in content and style. (As there are special problems in obtaining money from a professional venture capitalist, the topic is dealt with separately in Chapter 5.)

The kind of financial proposal which this chapter describes is relatively simple; it may be used when seeking any of the following three sources of funds: well-to-do family members or friends who might be sold on investing in your business; another small business operator who might be interested in a franchising arrangement with your business and willing to finance its expansion; a "factor" who may be interested in buying some of your customer accounts, thereby providing you with operating money.

Other topics this chapter will explore include the possibility of obtaining a line of credit from a supplier and the wisdom of leasing your capital facilities instead of buying them. The same simplified financial proposal can be used in convincing either a supplier or a leasing company that your business venture is sound. Remember, however, that though we have described the proposal as being simple, you can be sure that it will still require a number of hours to put together. The following elements should be included:

1. The estimated market for your product or service.
2. How you plan to reach that market.
3. Your financial plan (in other words, your business budget).
4. A brief description of your company and your managerial experience.
5. How much money (or other assets) you will need, when it will be paid back, and, most important, what the provider of funds will get in return for his financial support of your business.

As previously stated, a proposal addressed to the financial sources with which this chapter deals can be relatively simple and straightforward, and it should not cost much to prepare. In fact, this is the sort of formal presentation that your organization should be able to turn out from time to time as the business grows. If you don't feel personally qualified to produce one, enlist the help of your accountant and lawyer and keep their version for use as a model. Just be sure that the five key elements listed above are included.

Make no mistake—even if you won't be negotiating with "big-league" investors, your proposal must be *convincing*. You will find that all people who are a potential source of funds, whether those funds be substantial or not, share one characteristic: concern for the safety of their money. Your proposal, above all, must demonstrate that safety.

Money Obtained from Family or Friends

Traditionally, when a would-be business owner doesn't have enough wealth to finance a new venture alone, or if a small business has insufficient capital to be able to expand, the first thought is to borrow from family or friends. In every family circle or among every group of close acquaintances there is usually at least one person who "has money." However, the amount of help that you can expect depends directly on the kind of relationship that you have had with that person. (You may not be in a position to ask for money from anyone, or you just may not want to.) If you do plan to persuade a friend or a member of your family to invest in your company, it should still be done with the simplified proposal discussed above. You will find that the more businesslike you are the better, even though you know the person well.

The important thing to keep in mind is that financial help from a relative or friend is <u>often contingent upon participation in the business</u>. That can be a compelling reason to seek money elsewhere. Some of the drawbacks of managing a family-owned business were discussed at the end of Chapter 1. You may want to review those comments when deciding whether or not to ask a wealthy acquaintance or relative to invest in your business.

How Franchising Can Supply Financial Support

Some kinds of business ventures adapt well to franchising; others do not. If yours is the type that could attract franchise money, study the situation carefully to see if you would gain from such a maneuver.

First, it should be said that a business in the start-up stage is not likely to adapt well to franchising. Normally the firm must already be successfully operating, that is, it should be profitable and have a marketable product or service that is considered unique. Examples would include a pizza house with, say, a unique, popular tomato sauce. Or perhaps you have developed an effective technique for teaching students to play a musical instrument, the technique being original enough to be copyrighted or patented.

Whatever the situation, if you plan on franchising, your business should be a going concern so that you can demonstrate convincing economic viability. Under those circumstances, you may very well be able to find a franchising investor who is willing to pay for permission to sell your item at a branch location or to expand into new territory. The prime factors here will be the investor's money plus your know-how and your product or service. Terms commonly used in a typical franchise agreement are:

Franchisor—you (and your company) with your experience as well as ownership of the franchised product or service.

Franchisee—the investor who wants to reap some of the benefits from the business you have started, by opening a branch in a new location.

The System—what the franchisee will distribute when the Agreement is carried out. This includes not only the product or service but also the operating procedures and any trade secrets.

The Agreement—the legally binding licensing arrangement which specifies the financial relationship between the two parties, the technical details of the System, the geographic boundaries, the time period, and all other aspects of the contract between the franchisor and franchisee.

The availability of additional funds is the prime advantage franchising offers. It can free you from the need to find any other source of capital or to invest any more of your own money in business expansion. However, there are several potential drawbacks to franchising that you should know about:

• As franchisor, you must be able to control the basic managerial practices of the franchisee. After all, his operation may reflect negatively on the overall reputation of your product or service, and unless specifications for control of the franchisee's business conduct are carefully written into the Agreement, he may ignore your control efforts. The franchisee will be fully aware that you have already used, or planned the use of, the money he has invested with you and so would be most reluctant to sever the relationship.

• As owner of the franchise, you will be obliged to train the key employees of any investor who enters into a franchise with you. Also, you must expect that a new franchisee will be inexperienced and will therefore depend for some time on your advice and support. The training and follow-up will be time consuming, but you must expect to have to do it.

• A franchisee will be highly profit-oriented, since his own livelihood will be at stake, and as a result, he is likely to resist your attempts to control his operation, even though you may consider them justifiable. This will be especially true if there is the possibility of extra cost to him. The result is that you will have to deal much more diplomatically with a franchisee than you would with your own employees. Persuasion, rather than direction, is the best approach.

• For all the above reasons, you are likely to find it desirable to set up formal operating procedures and written standards for the franchisee to follow. Such a step often involves considerable effort and/or expense, and can represent a serious drawback to franchising.

Having reviewed these demerits, you will be in a better position to evaluate this method of obtaining money. Many small but growing businesses have experimented with franchising with good and bad results. Before deciding one way or the other, however, there are other sources of funds you should consider.

Arranging for a Factoring Company to Buy Your Receivables

Once your business is in operation, the matter of extending credit to customers will come up. Almost all business establishments do it; you should strongly consider doing it too. However, this means that your operating funds will have to be stretched to cover the period between when a customer buys and when he pays. Also, it means that you will have to establish a collecting activity within your business, designating someone to follow up to make sure your customers pay. Finally, the practice of extending credit always involves partial payments, which means you must set up a separate file for each credit customer and record each time he pays part of his balance.

These problems can be eliminated if you sell your receivables to a "factor" (also called a factoring company). The factoring company will then take over the collecting activity and the bookkeeping, and you will get paid much sooner. Of course, there is a catch to this agreement—the discount the factor gets when he buys your customer accounts. This discount will normally exceed 10 percent, and therefore is a significant cost element to be considered. Nonetheless, soliciting the services of a factoring company is a common way for many small businesses to cover their credit sales.

The most common form of factoring consists of an outright sale of receivables to the factor. Normally, each credit transaction is transferred shortly after the customer has signed a sales contract with you. You notify the customer that the factoring company has taken over his account and will be collecting the payments, and the factor pays you the (discounted) proceeds for the sale.

A second kind of factoring has begun to appear in recent years as the result of (a) bad debt losses experienced by many factors, and (b) business resistance to the higher discount charged by factors to offset those losses. Under this arrangement, the factor holds back part of the proceeds until he collects the total amount due from the account he purchased from you. Also, if the account goes sour and the factor is unable to collect, he will demand the remainder of the settlement from your business. This method would be obviously less advantageous except that the factor's discount rate is usually lower because he assumes less risk. Be sure to compare factor discount rates if you decide to sell your customer accounts, and then pick the form of factoring that's best for you.

As you may have gathered, there are both advantages to be enjoyed and disadvantages to be suffered when you make an arrangement with a factoring company. The advantages center around the ready availability of operations financing and the elimination of credit bookkeeping. In effect, by factoring, all of your sales are converted to a cash basis. This may be worth quite a bit to you, particularly if you have considerable working capital tied up in inventory and not enough money available to carry customer accounts.

The disadvantages are primarily the discount the factor charges and the probability that your customers will assume your business is short of cash. If you are contending against strong competition, where the price of your product or service has already been subject to heavy undercutting, you may not be able to afford to deal with a factor. The middle of a price war is not exactly the best time to take on more costs. On the other hand, all forms of financing have their costs. Weighing factoring costs versus expenses associated with alternate sources of money will indicate whether dealing with the former is good business.

One final objection may be your reluctance to indicate to customers that you have accepted this kind of financial help. Some business operators simply can't bring themselves to reveal any weakness, and factoring, they feel, is indeed a sign of some desperation. So, if your personal pride or business prestige would be injured, then selling receivables to a factoring company is not for you.

Operations Financed by a Supplier

Depending on the kind of business you operate, there may be a good chance of obtaining considerable financial assistance from one or more of your company's major suppliers. There are, however, four principal restrictions to keep in mind with this type of financing.

1. The funding normally obtainable would be available mostly to maintain your operations, as distinguished from improving your physical plant. In other words, capital equipment is normally not provided by a supplier unless it is needed for his own product. A juice dispenser might be provided for a soda fountain, but a cash register probably would not.

The motivation behind any extension of credit by a supplier is obviously to stimulate purchases of *his* products or services by your company. There is much greater likelihood of obtaining this kind of funding if your firm is already a going concern. Start-up credit for a small business is generally not provided except under special circumstances such as a highly competitive market for the supplier.

2. The kinds of products or service lines where this par-

ticular financial support is available are generally those designed for mass distribution. Seasonal clothing designs or brand-name food products are typical. Common characteristics of businesses that may anticipate financial help from suppliers are (a) high volume and (b) low unit prices. If your business is in low-demand specialty goods or "big ticket" items, there is only a remote possibility that any of your suppliers will offer financial help.

3. To the extent that it is legal, a supplier who provides credit to you will attempt to "freeze out" his competition. However, if that is the case, you may be able to use that supplier's inclination as a lever to bargain for the greatest possible support from other competitor suppliers.

4. Your inventory turnover must be fairly rapid (about 30 to 60 days) if you expect to operate mostly on suppliers' money. By selling products within that time span, you'll be able to collect from the majority of your customers before your suppliers bill you for the items they financed.

If you can operate within these four limitations, you should be able to make effective use of one or more suppliers' lines of credit. (This procedure is also known as "buying on open credit" from a supplier.) It may well be the best and cheapest source of operating funds that you will be able to find.

During the negotiating process with a potential supplier, it is appropriate to present a copy of your formal financial-assistance proposal. You will find that although almost any supplier will compete for your business as a "straight" customer, he will still be keenly interested in your approach to the use of his credit. The "professionalism" of your financing presentation will have a bearing on the upper limit of the credit a supplier is willing to extend.

Leasing Your Capital Facilities

You might consider it odd that a section on facilities leasing should be included as part of a chapter on financing. But stop to consider the many benefits your business can obtain through leasing various items.

• If you can lease it, you don't have to buy it. This enables you to stretch your capital by channeling more dollars into operating funds (working capital).

• Almost anything used by a business can be leased these days, including not only your building but the production equipment within it. Your delivery truck and company auto can be leased, and so can various store fixtures and even the office furniture and business machines.

• Lease payments are classed as business expenses and are deductible from your business income tax. In many cases, this deduction will exceed the depreciation cost which would be incurred if the item had been purchased. In any event, the lease payment comes out of "earnings before taxes," whereas that portion of the purchase price of a capital facility which has not yet been subject to depreciation becomes a reduction of after-tax profit when the item is eventually replaced.

• In some cases (but not all), a lease-purchase agreement can be negotiated so that a considerable part of the rental can be applied against an eventual purchase of the article. While the item is under lease, it is normally maintained by the owner. This means that repairs and occasionally modernizing can be had at no expense.

• When future needs are uncertain, or if the possibility of obsolescence is high, a lease plan will seem most attractive. With the advent of highly automated production equipment or office machinery, managers are even more likely to prefer to lease because of the good possibility that they will need to replace the items in a few years.

• The leasing of equipment may be used as a hedge against inflation so long as the present period of rapidly rising prices continues. The lease payments, spread over the term of the contract, become less significant as other costs go higher and higher.

With the above in mind, you can see that leasing capital facilities may well provide a financial benefit to your business, particularly as it passes through the start-up phase. Also, if your business begins to expand rapidly, the same advantages apply. Leasing production equipment is especially beneficial at this time when there are so many other demands on your limited supply of capital.

As usual, a few words of caution are in order. Leasing equipment can be a disadvantage to your business under certain conditions. Consider the following restrictions.

• Leasing is most profitable on a short-term basis. After about the fifth year, leasing becomes more expensive, compared to the remaining depreciation cost, for most kinds of equipment. This is true partly because of the reduced undepreciated value of purchased equipment more than five years old and partly because, as experience has shown, many kinds of equipment can be used beyond the period of depreciation. Such an item becomes available for use at no cost, for all intents and purposes.

• Usually the terms of the lease require that the manufacturer's supplies and accessories be used exclusively. In some cases, this material is more costly than products offered by competitor suppliers.

• Purchased equipment can be used overtime with no expense other than for maintenance and supplies. Some leased equipment carries an extra charge for overtime use, although the rate is generally lower than the regular rate.

• If equipment is purchased, it becomes an asset which you may trade in. Leased equipment does not offer this advantage; no equity in equipment can be derived from lease payments.

Insofar as the leasing of a *building* is concerned, the principal drawback could be your landlord's insertion of extra clauses into the lease that could either cost you money or make your business subject to a lawsuit. There are several areas to watch out for.

Percentage-of-business clause. This authorizes your landlord to claim a percentage of your business revenue over and above a base amount. If you are faced with such a clause, be sure that the following deductions are permitted from your gross revenue:

- Sales, excise, and use taxes.
- Returns or allowances given to customers.
- Finance charges (if any) added on the "cash sale" price.
- Payments for delivery or installation service.

Negligence clause. This stipulation may make your business liable for damage to the landlord's premises in the event of negligence on the part of you or your employees. If your lease contains this restriction, you can cover it in one of two ways:

- Take out a comprehensive fire and accident insurance policy; then, if there is negligence, the insurance company is liable, not your business.
- Persuade the landlord to include your business in *his* insurance policy.

Escalation-of-charges clause. This possibility may make your business liable for increases in building maintenance costs, utility costs, tax assessments, or other charges. Such a circumstance may result if the landlord's operating costs grow enough to cut into his profitability and he attempts to pass the burden on to you. There is generally no way to escape these charges except to move. If you prefer to stay put, make sure that your lease contains the following:

- A specification of the kinds of building maintenance or operating costs included in the lease and those which cannot be passed on.
- Precise description of the tax base or the tax year used in calculating the extra increment being charged to you.
- An allowance for part-time occupancy (less than a full year) in order to shield the business from any extra charges during your first months of occupancy.

No matter what kind of building or equipment you would consider leasing, the charges and/or restrictions inserted into the lease will depend to some extent on your business credentials. If considerable foresight and managing expertise are demonstrated by your financial proposal, the lessor will feel more secure in entering into the agreement, and as a result, there will probably be fewer penalty clauses to plague you when you finally sign the lease.

Conclusion

In reading this chapter, you may have concluded that finding financing causes more problems than any other aspect of managing a business. This isn't necessarily the case; however, it is important to be very selective in seeking "outside" funding. The next two chapters will suggest some other avenues leading toward a sound capital base. Read all of the material before you make up your mind as to the most feasible sources, and pay special attention to the various disadvantages and drawbacks. It is far better to find out about possible troubles through a book than from having gotten personally involved.

Without doubt, the small business owner who can set up and operate a company using only his own money is very lucky. Most businesses do not start that way, and there is no need to feel ashamed if you need financial help. On the other hand, the decisions you must make regarding this subject are likely to be among the most important you will ever face. So tackle it only after you've learned all you can. Make sure that your estimate of how much money your business will need is realistic, then go out and get it.

4

How to Obtain
Financial Help
from Your Banker

SAY you operate a small manufacturer's supply company specializing in the sale of various fastening devices. You do much of the selling and have concentrated on three "house accounts," which are the mainstay of your company. One day, while calling on the most important of these accounts, you run into Jim Black, the vice-president of manufacturing. You are invited to his office and are informed that they have decided to open a fabricating plant in Millville, a small city 30 miles away. Black looks you squarely in the eye and asks if he can count on you to supply all the necessary fasteners for this new plant. He also indicates that you should be able to fill any of the new plant's emergency needs "on 15 minutes notice." The implication is that if you won't make a commitment to satisfy all his requirements, he'll be on the lookout for another supplier. Also, he wants an answer "yesterday."

At this point, how nice it would be to be able to go to the phone, call your banker, and tell him you're considering opening a small branch in Millville. As a result of your talk with Black, you estimate a guaranteed demand for about 50 percent of the potential deliveries from this proposed new warehouse. You also project a need to borrow approximately $15,000 for at least 12 months so that you can lease a building, stock a beginning inventory of fasteners, and buy a second-hand delivery truck. It would be even nicer if the banker had so much confidence in you that he would tell you to come in to his office tomorrow, as "there won't be any trouble with the loan"!

What's the connection between this fictitious event and your business? It's very simple: the time to *prepare* to borrow money from a bank is well in advance of when you actually need it. You may never experience the equivalent of a Jim Black with his new plant in Millville. However, sooner or later, your business will suddenly develop a need for more money than you can put your hands on. You may need the funds in order to seize some unusual opportunity, or to ward off disaster. Whatever the reason, the need will occur. You can count on it. So, *today,* you should begin to lay the foundations for that bank loan of the future.

Perhaps your business is presently operating without sufficient cash reserves. Many small businesses are started in an undercapitalized condition and function successfully until some emergency cash requirement catches up with them. When the day of reckoning arrives, the owner frequently doesn't have sufficient personal funds to be able to supply the needed cash out of his own resources. However, if the appropriate preliminary steps have already been taken, the owner should be able to obtain a loan from a bank without also having to get acquainted with his banker in the process.

Getting to Know Your Banker in Advance

You should start to get on good terms with your banker as soon as you open a checking account for the business. In fact, the future potential availability of commercial loans should be an important consideration when choosing the business's bank in the first place. Bear in mind that banks vary in their willingness to make loans depending upon the characteristics of their customers. Often, banks with considerable "personal" business (wage-earner or consumer accounts) will have more money to lend than banks that deal largely with business concerns. This is because nonbusiness customers do not require the large individual loans that commercial and industrial accounts generally ask for.

Direct contact with a banker who knows you and has an interest in your business can be beneficial in other ways. For example, when you need a quick credit check on a potential customer, he may give you that information over the telephone. He may also provide free advice on investment opportunities or market conditions. There are literally dozens of ways a banker can serve his clients in addition to making loans. Thus, one of your aims should be to cultivate a friend among the loan officers at your bank, someone who trusts you and in whom you can confide.

Another objective is to ensure that the official is aware of your unique banking needs. If he is not already familiar with your business, your job is to acquaint him or her with it, as well as to explain your methods of operation. An even more important task is to prove that you are a competent and progressive manager.

Earning Your Banker's Respect

Building a permanent relationship with your bank is chiefly a matter of earning the respect of the loan official with whom you deal. You can do that and build a reputation for good character and integrity by conducting your banking affairs in a logical manner. In this, several gestures are essential: (1) show good faith, (2) provide the official with full financial data, and (3) discuss your future business plans.

Show good faith. Good faith is the single most important factor that will assist you in your daily dealings with a banker. A very important way of establishing trust is to keep the official informed on all the developments of your business, good or bad. It is especially important to do this *after* you have borrowed money. If at some point you can't meet the payment schedule and you try to hide that fact, it can only create a bad impression at the bank.

Provide financial data. Furnishing financial facts about your business can help the banker to be sure that you are a competent manager—one who operates his business profitably and keeps it in sound financial condition. So, right from the start give him your *complete* financial picture. Provide copies of your profit and loss statements, balance sheets, flow of funds, and cost and budget statements. This should be done soon after opening up a bank account—and long before you feel the need for a loan. Such financial reports will mean a great deal to your banker, who will keep them in his file on your firm. Bear in mind that supplying a complete statement of your firm's finances helps to build your reputation for integrity. Lending officers are suspicious of data that is incomplete or which is turned in grudgingly. Such questionable information can create a serious handicap in the future for the small business person who seeks quick approval of a loan.

Discuss future plans. When your banker knows about your future intentions, he can develop a better understanding of what your anticipated financial needs will be. Then he can offer more specific advice and suggest ways in which the bank can help you to meet those needs. As previously explained, the time to give him this information is well before you expect to need the money. Such planning offers another good way to build strong relations with your banker. His respect is certain to be substantial for small businessmen who plan because there are so many who do not. For example, a nonplanner often runs into financial trouble when his sales expand rapidly. The reason: the cash flow generated by the increased sales is not sufficient to pay for increased stocks, parts inventory, and other current expenses. Thus, a business owner who has no specific plans gets into trouble even when he is successful in generating a lot more business. In every case, bankers much prefer to deal with a business that anticipates its financial needs.

Information Your Bank Will Need

The principal function of any bank is to help service the financial needs of the community and at the same time to generate a profit for its stockholders. Furthermore, since banks are charged by regulatory agencies with protecting the deposits of their customers, it is necessary to maintain adequate capital reserves as well as to achieve efficiency in their operations. Banks must also exercise sound judgment in setting up their lending policies.

The primary job of a bank lending officer is to make profitable loans for his bank. To do this, he must obtain enough information to intelligently evaluate every loan request. When the time arrives for you to apply for a loan, your friend, the lending officer, in analyzing your application must know the amount of money you require, the purpose of the loan, your expected source of funds for repayment, and the availability of collateral.

How Your Loan Request Will Be Analyzed and Evaluated

Most lending officers employ the well-known technique of asking probing questions of a prospective borrower. Such questions will probably take one of the following forms:

"How much money do you want?" It is important to demonstrate sound business judgment in supporting the requested amount, so be sure that you request neither too much nor too little, and be able to show why you are asking for that specific sum.

"What is the purpose of the loan?" The loan should make

good business sense, that is, it should contribute to increasing the profits of your business in some demonstrable way. This is very important since it provides an indication of the quality of your judgment.

"What is your primary source of money for repayment?" You must be able to identify precisely your future sources of funds. Short-term operational loans, which are often called self-liquidating loans, should be repaid from the conversion into cash of the assets being purchased (usually inventories). If such conversion is delayed, these loans must then be repaid from the general earnings of the business. A longer-term loan for the purchase of a capital asset should be repayable from the (forecasted) profits generated by that particular asset. As an example, if you run a machine shop and want to purchase a new computer-operated machine that could increase production by 30 percent, then profits derived from the greater production would be indicated as the source of repaying the loan needed to pay for the machine. These loans also may involve a mortgage where the asset itself is used as security for the loan.

"What is your collateral (or secondary source of repayment) in case your business fails to generate the anticipated funds to repay the loan?" A secondary repayment source may be guaranteed for repayment of a loan issued in the name of the business. In banking terms, this is known as a "general business guarantee." Sometimes, however, the actual net worth of operation is so limited that its "general guarantee" has insufficient value. This is frequently the problem of new businesses. In such a case, the personal net worth of the owner may be substituted if his personal guarantee adds significantly to that of the business.

In the event that a general or a personal guarantee is not sufficient, a list of collateral owned either by the business or by you personally can also be specifically assigned to the bank to support a loan. Examples of collateral your business may own are:

Accounts receivable.
Inventory.

Equipment and machinery.
Contracts receivable.
Real estate.

Examples of collateral that may be owned by you personally are:

Life insurance policy with cash surrender value.
Savings account.
Municipal, government, or corporate bonds.
Time certificates of deposit.
Marketable securities.
Real estate.

"Do you have sufficient life insurance and business insurance to cover any contingency?" Your banker will understand that as a businessperson, life insurance is very important to you. When considering your request for a loan, he will be particularly interested in the amount and type of insurance coverage. There is one sort of life insurance coverage that, if you die while manager of your business, provides for the disposition of the firm according to your stated wishes. This is called "key man" insurance and it is important for a variety of reasons, both to the estate of the deceased and to the continuation of the business. It is also of great significance to a bank in considering your request for a loan.

In the case of a proprietorship, this life insurance enables debts to be satisfied without forcing the executor of the estate to "invade" the principal assets of the business to settle creditors' claims. In the case of "key man" partnership insurance, the beneficiary of the life insurance policy is likely to be the other partner or partners. There, the insurance benefits provide the surviving partner(s) with the funds to purchase the portion of the company owned by the deceased. In the case of a small corporation where the stock is owned by only a few individuals, the corporation itself may be named beneficiary of all of the "key man" policies carried by the owners. If one of them dies, the insurance payment can then provide the corporation with funds sufficient to purchase and then hold the stock of the deceased owner, without reducing the liquidity of the firm.

In addition, any business that is borrowing money should have sufficient "casualty" insurance to protect all its business property. This insurance should cover robbery, fire, personal injury, and business interruption.

Your Banking Relationship Summarized

Every bank lending officer, through experience and training, develops his or her own style and approach and most have a personal preference for certain criteria when analyzing loan applications. Therefore, it is impossible to know exactly what your lending officer will be looking for when a loan application is entered by your business. General business conditions, as well as particular situations within the bank itself, will always have some influence on the acceptability of loan applications. Factors such as these are clearly beyond your control.

However, as we have stressed in these pages, you should establish a good relationship with a bank official well before the actual application, in order to smooth the process as much as possible. Then you should be prepared to answer the banker's questions as explained above. You may also be required to utilize the services of a CPA or an attorney. Some lending officers are reluctant to deal with a business that does not employ these independent professionals, and in fact this is the general policy of many banks. The accountant whom you hire can act as a disinterested third party in reviewing your records and operations, evaluating your business, its financial standing, and so on. Your attorney would be available to cover any of a number of legal contingencies, depending upon your kind of business. To pay the fees charged for either or both of these services is somewhat like paying insurance premiums—it's expensive, but worth it when funds are being sought from a bank.

Types of Bank Financing

Don't get the impression that negotiating a bank loan for your business will be almost automatic. It won't be, at least not the first few times. Also, the purpose of the loan will have a great deal to do with your bank's willingness to lend. It is much easier to negotiate a bank loan to promote growth than to cover a loss. So let us hope that the encounters with your banker will mostly be for money you need to expand sales and earn more profits.

In any case, remember that the bank will make money every time you borrow. If your past repayment record is good, your banker probably will be glad to see you when you apply for a new loan. He will *want* to lend money to help you succeed, because your interest payments will become his revenue.

When considering the kinds of business loans that banks generally make, you'll find that there are several types. The reason for the variety is simply that bank loan officers use different vehicles to assure that their portfolio of loans is "balanced." Some of these are described below.

Self-Liquidating Loans

This form is utilized (a) when the borrower has good financial standing, and (b) when the borrowed funds are intended to be used for working capital or to acquire assets capable of being converted quickly into cash. For example, a 90-day loan may be taken out to acquire retail inventory prior to the height of the Christmas buying season. This is a very common type of commercial lending; in fact, self-liquidating loans are the mainstay of business for many banks.

Capital Loans

Sometimes loans are made for the purpose of buying an asset of long-term value, for instance, a delivery truck. Such items are known as *fixed assets* or *capital facilities,* and loans made to acquire them are called *capital loans.* (This subject will be discussed at some length in Chapter 8.) Capital loans are often secured by the bank by taking out a mortgage on the asset being purchased. When this is not done, the bank simply relies on the general earning power of the borrower or on a good credit history with respect to previous loans.

Inventory Loans

In the event that a bank requires collateral of some kind to secure a loan for working capital, inventory on hand can sometimes be used as backing. "Floor planning" of major inventory items (such as home appliances or automobiles) is one approach commonly employed for loans to retail establishments or auto dealers. Under this plan, the article(s) pledged as collateral must be located in a specific area in the borrower's showroom at the time the loan is made, and are then checked monthly by the bank until repayment of the loan is completed. If one or more of these collateral items are sold by the borrower during the loan period, a substitute article of equal or greater value must be pledged instead and displayed in the prescribed location in the showroom.

Another type of inventory loan is based on a bonded warehouse receipt. In this case, the bank takes a security interest in goods stored by the borrower *under bond* in an established warehouse where goods are commonly held in sealed storage. The goods cannot be moved or the seal broken until the loan is paid off. The warehouse receipt serves as a guarantee that the material will remain secure, and it is turned over to the bank for retention during the loan period.

From the bank's viewpoint, this approach to lending is less desirable than a self-liquidating loan because of the paper work involved. Borrowers, on the other hand, are not necessarily inconvenienced unless the inventory used as collateral is so scarce as to hamper day-to-day operations. The higher rate of interest charged by the bank is the principal drawback of inventory loans.

Accounts-Receivable Loans

This type of loan is considered less risky by banks than an inventory loan mostly because receivables are only one step away from conversion into cash. However, a bank generally will not advance more than 75–80 percent of the face value of the pledged accounts. (This is a protection against "bad debts.") Customers may or may not be notified that their accounts have been assigned. If notified, they usually are instructed to make payments directly to the lending bank. If not notified, the customers continue to pay the borrower who promptly turns such payments over to the bank. Most borrowers prefer the latter approach, since customers then are not aware that their account has been pledged to secure a loan. Borrowing is still considered an embarrassing weakness by some business people, although this attitude seems to be disappearing.

Loans Secured by Other Types of Collateral

In some situations, a borrower may have to pledge various assets, including business property or even his own personal possessions in order to secure a loan. As a general rule, such collateral is considered to be the least desirable of all. This is true from the standpoint of both parties. The lending bank will be reluctant because assets assigned under this arrangement often have a resale value considerably below original cost, and the borrower will usually prefer almost any other arrangement than to be forced to assign his own business equipment and other assets as collateral.

One method that is generally more acceptable to both parties is for the borrower to pledge the cash surrender value of an insurance policy on his or her life. When such an arrangement is made, the borrower turns the insurance policy over to the bank along with a properly notarized "assignment" form supplied by the insurance company. If the borrower dies during the term of the loan, the bank has first claim on the proceeds of the policy, although only for the amount of the loan. If the borrower defaults on the loan, the bank may obtain settlement from the cash surrender value of the policy. After the loan is repaid, all documents are returned to the borrower and the policy "assignment" is cancelled.

Term Loans

There is often a need for "intermediate" credit—part way between a typical short-term loan and a long-term business financing arrangement, such as borrowing venture capital or taking on another equity partner. This type of lending is for a period of at least several years and is referred to as *term lending* or *installment lending*. The latter name indicates a characteristic common with most longer loan plans—regular installment payments against the capital. (By way of contrast, most short-term loans are repayable in one lump sum at maturity.)

Term loans may be made either to increase working capital or, more commonly, to finance a major expansion of capital facilities. In any case, they represent a more complex form of borrowing than a regular short-term loan. Sometimes more than one bank is involved, especially if the loan is rather sizable. The borrower usually agrees not to incur any other indebtedness until the term loan is paid off, and may also pledge to retain some current assets at a level higher than a stipulated amount and to restrict the distribution of dividends. All of these provisions signify the same thing: a term loan is considered somewhat risky, and the bank will usually try to protect it with as many safeguards as possible.

Although interest on any bank loan is always a significant business expense, your major consideration should be *what you can do with the borrowed money.* If you can increase the sales or the profitability of your company, the interest cost of a bank loan is really no more important than any other element in the expense of doing business. Likewise, if you can outrun your competition by using the proceeds of a bank loan, the long-range benefits can be very worthwhile. Even when you are borrowing to consolidate past debts, the new loan may give you enough breathing room to enable your business to get a fresh start.

The most important aspect of bank financing, therefore, is *not the expense but the flexibility* that your business can derive as the result of an intelligent borrowing plan.

Small Business Administration Financing

The federal Small Business Administration (SBA) was established by Congress in 1953 to assist and counsel and to provide financial aid to people like you and to businesses like yours. It has helped thousands of small companies to get started or grow. It may be of major benefit when you want to borrow for expansion or conversion of facilities, when you want to invest in inventory, buy more equipment, and so on. The question is, how can you get an SBA loan?

According to regulations, you must seek private financing from a bank, insurance company, or some other lending institution before applying to the SBA. Only after you have been turned down by a private lender are you eligible for SBA help (if you live in a city of 200,000 or more your bid must have been rejected by at least two lenders). However, requests for loans are refused in more cases than you might think, especially when businesses are just getting started or when the economy is weak.

In the event that you are denied a direct loan by a bank, you are entitled to ask that bank to make the loan under the SBA Loan Guarantee Plan. Not all banks are willing to do this (even though it is to their advantage, since the SBA will guarantee up to 90 percent of the amount of the loan). However, by shopping around, you should be able to find a bank with a positive SBA loan policy. If not, write or contact your nearest SBA office, and they will help in the search.

Other forms of SBA assistance are (a) "participation" loans, where a bank and the SBA jointly make the loan; and

(b) "direct" loans, where the SBA provides all of the funds without any help from a bank. Both of these are harder to arrange than the guarantee plan. Your best bet is to try for an SBA guarantee loan.

Some qualifying remarks are in order so that you don't get the impression that Uncle Sam is waiting with an open wallet for you to ask for money. That isn't the case at all. An SBA loan must be arranged on a businesslike basis. In fact, the procedure for application is about the same as that which your bank would require if it were making a direct loan. You must:

- Have a good business reputation.
- Demonstrate that you can operate a business success-fully and show that the proposed loan can be repaid.
- Have enough other capital (or show that you have access to it) so that *with the SBA loan* the business will be on a sound financial basis.
- Have a sufficient personal stake in the business to be willing to stand a considerable period of low earnings (or even losses) before you turn the corner into Easy Street.

The principal difference between an SBA loan and a normal bank loan is that SBA assumes most of the risk. That is what may swing the deal for you if direct borrowing from a bank proves to be impossible.

Conclusion

Commercial banks are only one of a number of different kinds of lending institutions in this country. From your standpoint, however, their importance can hardly be over-stated. Ready availability of bank credit is absolutely crucial to most small businesses. The principal qualification from any bank's point of view is that a borrower should have enough earning power to repay a loan. But as long as you are honest and have a good business reputation, you can expect to have very little trouble in dealing with the bank of your choice *if your business is profitable.*

You should realize, however, that a few other intangible factors can influence your banker's decision. Some of these may not be apparent to you, or, even if you are aware of them, it may be difficult to evaluate their importance. First, consider internal bank concerns. Most banks have lending "targets," meaning that if they are already overcommitted in their commercial loan portfolios, they will be less likely to greet your application with great enthusiasm. The opposite would be true if the banks' available funds from savings accounts are temporarily excessive. The growth policy of a bank will also influence its aggressiveness in favoring new loans. A conservative policy would dictate low-risk loans, whereas an expansionistic growth policy would have the reverse effect. Finally, the length of your prior association with your bank and the amount of money that you normally keep on deposit may have considerable impact.

Second, you should keep in mind external economic factors. Many things beyond your control, and also beyond the control of your bank, can be influential. Current environmental concerns may be decisive, particularly in the case of a loan request from a business whose processes, say, pollute the air or water. The present energy crisis may adversely influence a loan application to open up a new filling station. The current volume of the nation's money supply operates continually to force interest rates up or down; the cost of borrowing is thus affected by decisions made by officials in Washington, D.C.

Regardless of any of the above factors, the long-run success of your business will depend in large measure on your skill in dealing with your banker. Whenever any business forecasts or experiences an insufficient cash flow from internally generated sources, short- or long-term borrowing becomes necessary. How, where, and why you decide to borrow are therefore matters of great significance. This chapter has offered some tips on how to do the right thing at the right time to get the most help from your banker.

5

How to Attract
"Venture Capital"
for Your Plan

THIS chapter concerns your potential relationship with a rather unusual type of business entrepreneur called a *venture capitalist*. Such an individual is in business for one purpose only—to sell the use of his or her money at the highest possible return with the lowest possible risk. Not many people have ever met a venture capitalist, at least not many who own or operate a small business. That's because

- There aren't very many venture capitalists except in the largest cities.
- Venture capitalists are usually individuals of considerable wealth, and their contacts are confined to circles of power and influence.
- It is often necessary for a venture capitalist to move

around a good deal to check out various possible investments.

- Many times it isn't an individual person at all but rather a *venture capitalist company* you'd be dealing with, and its employees aren't true venture capitalists in their own right.

However, all venture capitalists (whether a company or a person) possess a common trait that may help you find and get acquainted with one of them. That characteristic is an unabashed attraction to the lure of a big payoff. They are invariably drawn to new ideas or new products; they always want to get into a promising business "on the ground floor" so that they can help make it grow while making good money. That is your ticket: if your deal sounds profitable enough, you may be able to arrange to meet with a venture capitalist. If your business can demonstrate the potential for substantial earnings and growth, you might also be able to form a long-term association with one of these investors.

Not every rich man or woman is a venture capitalist. Many individuals with money are content to clip their coupons and cash their dividend checks, and they seldom take an investment gamble. These people generally are not the sort of investor you would attract even with a highly profitable venture. In contrast, a venture capitalist would probably be bored keeping his money tied up in a portfolio of investments in common stocks or corporate bonds. The return isn't great enough.

It will be instructive to study Table 2, indicating the various percentages of return on investment that different degrees of investment risk are commonly expected to provide. Pay particular attention to the "reward percentage" column for venture financing, keeping in mind the following formula:

$$\text{ROI reward percentage} = \frac{\text{asset appreciation} + \text{annual revenue}}{\text{total investment}}$$

Table 2. Scale of risks and expected rewards for different investments.

Type of Investment	*Reward Percentage*
Government bonds (federal or state)	3.5–4.5
Corporate bonds (publicly owned company)	4–5
Savings account (bank or savings and loan)	5–5.5
Income-producing common stock (publicly owned company)	5–6.5
Growth common stock (publicly owned company)	9–12
Speculative common stock (unlisted but established company)	13–18
Venture financing, 3rd-stage company (company is beginning to be profitable— ready for significant expansion of capital)	25–30 *
Venture financing, 2nd-stage company (company is not yet profitable, but has some output and established customers)	35–40 *
Venture financing, 1st-stage company (company is organized, has "pilot" product or service, and has made deliveries)	40–50 *
Venture financing, start-up stage company (company being organized or in first year, with prototype product or service and possibly with customer orders)	50+ *

* Most venture-financed businesses will not earn the desired reward percentage for a number of years. Therefore, these percentages must be annualized as follows:

$$\text{Annualized reward percentage} = \frac{E + V}{n}$$

where E = total earnings, V = appreciated value of investment, and n = number of years the investment is held. Keep in mind that many venture capitalists or their companies will want to liquidate their holdings in from five to seven years after acquisition.

If the high returns expected for venture financing have set you back a bit, it isn't surprising. However, that is what you can expect to give up if a venture capitalist agrees to invest in your business. It may have been your original idea, but the dollars will be mostly his. Furthermore, in order to minimize the risk, the venture capitalist (person or company) is very likely to want to take part in the active management of your business. Frequently, this will be to your advantage, since most successful venture capitalists can contribute considerable business know-how along with their money. At any rate, the scale of rewards that a venture capitalist will require in exchange for providing financial backing will always be quite substantial.

Now that you understand what may be involved, are you still interested in attracting large-scale venture capital? If not, your possible sources of funding will be limited to those described in the two previous chapters. But if you are prepared to have an "outsider" share in the actual running of your company and to receive a very sizable part of the proceeds, then you have taken the first step toward large-scale business success. For, indeed, if you truly want to found a large company and to earn a great deal of money, it will take more than a good product or service line and lots of hard work. You'll need substantial capital plus a means of making contact with influential people and large, potential customers. The right venture capitalist can supply all of that for you; and that's what makes venture financing a good deal for you despite the large profit "rake-off."

The Appeal of Your Product or Service

Up to this point, the discussion of how you would find a venture capitalist has assumed that you are justified in hunting for one. In other words, nothing has been mentioned with regard to your company organization or the product or service that will provide the "bait." However, these are very important factors and there are a few things about them that would normally be required by a venture capitalist.

First, let's talk about the kind of a business that would probably *not* be of any interest. A hamburger stand or fried-chicken outlet is unlikely to qualify. A plumbing supply dealership would also have very little appeal. The problem in these cases is insufficient volume. Take any business heading in the yellow pages of the telephone book: if there are a good many listings already under that particular heading, a venture capitalist would be unlikely to consider financing another one. The reason is the same—too much competition and not enough potential return. This is not to say that you should abandon the idea of going into or retaining a business which has a lot of competition. If such a line is most compatible with your interests or is what your experience best qualifies you for, then stick with it. If others can make a living pursuing it, you probably can too. (The remaining chapters will be of much help to you in doing that.)

But, at this point, we are talking about financing a business with the prospect of making a lot of money. The potential return must be enough to be attractive to an entrepreneur who is already wealthy and who very likely also has an interest in several other successful companies. Not many new or existing business ventures will have enough appeal.

Take another key characteristic of a good investment for a venture capitalist, that of low "capital intensity." The term "capital intensity" is a technical financial phrase which refers to necessary capital facilities that an ongoing business must use in its operations, that is, its building, tools, and equipment. For instance, the Polaroid Corporation is a highly capital-intensive company. However, that company only gradually acquired the impressive capital plant it now utilizes. Suppose that you have applied for a patent for a different kind of self-developing film, but which could be used in Polaroid cameras. To produce and distribute that film would require overnight financing of a company that would be on about the same high level of capital intensity as Polaroid. Continuing the example, suppose that on the other hand you had developed a process that could be used for converting wood fiber into attractive shipping and display cartons for Polaroid. The technology would be simpler, and as a result, your company would be less capital-intensive. Also you could offer the same kinds of cartons to Polaroid's competition, or to pocket calculator manufacturers, to CB radio distributors and so on. It is obvious that the second deal would be much more attractive to a venture capitalist.

There are two other characteristics a product or service must have to appeal to a venture capitalist. These are high *salability* and *profitability*. You might want to compare some of the following attributes of good marketability and profit potential with what your company has to offer now or what it may offer in the future:

- The product or service should have a low "output" cost. This is usually consistent with a minimum need for capital intensity, and enhances profitability.
- If yours is a manufactured product, it is desirable that the item can be subcontracted in whole or in part. Again, this quality is compatible with low capital intensity.
- The product or service should be readily salable at a reasonable price that still provides a substantial profit. This marketability characteristic depends directly on the degree of product or service acceptance and also on the level of your competition.
- You should be able to make a convincing case that the product or service satisfies a "felt" need. This marketing advantage would obviate the necessity of creating a demand; the only remaining task would be to convince customers that your product or service fills that need.

What to Do Before Seeking Venture Capital

There are a number of "positioning" maneuvers that you should consider before beginning an active campaign to obtain venture capital for your company. All of these preparatory steps will take time; some may be expensive; any of them may tip the balance in your favor with a potential investor. Actually, the benefit of carrying them out is twofold: they maximize the attractiveness of your deal, and they reduce the expected reward percentage as much as possible, allowing you to keep more of the future profits. This can only be accomplished by reducing the potential overall risk of the project.

Refer again to Table 2 showing the various reward percentages that a new company must give up in order to get venture financing. Note in particular the difference between the start-up-stage and second-stage percentages. If you can advance your business as far as the second stage before seeking venture financing, you can expect to be able to keep a greater share of the company's interest as well as its earnings.

The following tactical steps are recommended for most small businesses in the early (prefinanced) stage of development:

1. Assemble the core of a balanced management team. Particular attention should be paid to recruiting talent which is qualified in general management and in finance. (It is assumed that either marketing know-how or technical or scientific competence will automatically be present within the company, since one or another of these talents usually provides the impetus for organizing a highly profitable new business in the first place.) A well-balanced management is absolutely essential when a venture capitalist begins to evaluate your proposal.

2. Make realistic cash-flow projections extending at least three years in advance. (The technique for doing this is discussed in Chapter 2.) Such projections should be developed on a strictly "no frills" basis. A sure way to discourage a potential investor is to plan sizable expenditures for luxury offices or to project big bonuses for key personnel. There will be time for such luxuries after the business gets over its early growing pains. And last, you should also provide convincing evidence that your business has been or will continue to be able to live by those cash-flow projections. This will mostly

depend on you personally—your life style, your integrity, your motivation, and so on.

3. Determine a realistic "breakeven" point, expressed in dollars of sales. (The way to do this is explained in Chapter 7.) Note that this step does not insist upon earning a profit. To expect immediate profitability is too much to ask for most small but promising companies. Instead, this "breakeven" determination simply establishes the sales level at which profits are anticipated.

4. Try hard to secure at least one order from a major customer, or, even better, begin to make deliveries against such an order. This is the best possible way to establish an initial business track record, from the viewpoint of venture financing. It proves, first, that your product or service generates demand, and second, that the company can take steps "on its own" to fill such demand.

If you can go into the market for venture capital armed with accomplishments such as those described above, you will have a solid base for bargaining. The only missing ingredient will be completion of your actual financing proposal, but even that will benefit greatly from the advance steps you have taken.

Preparing Your Formal Financing Proposal

You should regard a financial proposal strictly as a selling tool. It must sell you and your product or service. Always keep in mind, as you go through the labor of preparing this instrument (or having it prepared by a professional), that any venture capitalist will require plenty of convincing. Thus, four important principles must be kept in mind: (1) clarity of presentation, (2) brevity, (3) overall credibility of the proposal, and (4) a positive approach.

Before elaborating on these principles, it is worth mentioning that the way in which all of them are blended into the text of the plan will reflect its professionalism. Your proposal must not only make sense, but also indicate judgment and good taste in describing what you plan to do.

Clarity of Presentation

The potential investor will want to know *exactly* what you plan to do, what market you foresee for your product or service, how much money you expect to need, how it will be repaid, and so on. This may sound easy to describe, but it isn't at all. Several different drafts should be made, aimed at providing a clear explanation. Let someone else review the presentations and then use his or her advice in preparing the final version.

Brevity

It is well to remember that a successful venture capitalist can be very busy; if so, he is not likely to be favorably impressed by a lengthy proposal. What you have to offer should be complete but concise. An attention-getting short version of the proposal should be included as a preface to the more detailed information. (If the abbreviated section is sufficiently interesting, an investor will feel much better about wading through the more complete treatment.)

Overall Credibility of the Proposal

The burden of proof will be on you to show that the organization is competent and that it can do what you are proposing. This is most important, since lack of experience can scare off any investor. The key points (discussed below) to be included in your proposal should be dealt with carefully and specifically. Vague generalities will not suffice. Keep in mind that the potential venture capitalist will be a financier at heart, and that he will be impressed by numbers. In other words, include as many graphs and tables and other hard data as possible.

Positive Approach

One of the worst things you can do in preparing a proposal is to project a totally neutral attitude. On the contrary, you should be optimistic, bursting with confidence. After all, if you don't believe completely in your deal, who will? So always use the word "will" instead of "might," "when" instead of "if," "surely" instead of "possibly," and so on. The finished proposal must represent your business fairly and accurately but, above all, *positively.*

Key Points to Be Covered by Your Proposal

Keeping the above principles in mind, let's turn our attention to the information that the proposal should contain. The items below can be, in effect, your "table of contents"; just fill in your own page numbers.

Brief summary of the proposal, stressing only the bare essentials of the "deal."

The idea or innovation on which the proposal is based.

The potential market which you propose to tap, including some sort of projected market analysis.

Your marketing plans, depicting the strategy and tactics that you plan to carry out to reach that market.

Your financial plans, describing how much money you require, how you plan to spend it, and how much return you expect.

Key management personnel, indicating who they are, their background and experience, and their assigned responsibility with your company.

The deal you are offering or are prepared to accept, stating in specific terms what you need and what you offer in return.

The art of creating a proposal containing this information may tax your personal abilities as well as those of your associates. Don't be surprised to find that you are dissatisfied with the first version and perhaps even the second or third. And don't worry—there are professionals who can polish your material, and they are generally worth the fee they charge. However, if you decide to subscribe to such a service be sure to take an active part in reviewing the final draft. Below is a checklist of what you should look for in the finished product, whether it's produced by you or by someone hired by you.

- Is there a brief but accurate description of the technical details of your product or service?
- Have your business objectives been spelled out? In other words, are there accurate descriptions of your sales, costs, and profit goals?
- Has your intended geographic market been properly described? Is there a good explanation for having chosen that particular area?
- Is your timetable for growth and increased profitability clearly set forth?
- Have your major competitors been named and discussed?
- Is the necessary capital equipment described in terms of both quantity and technical specifications?
- Are your building or office space needs properly described? Is your personnel staffing plan clearly outlined?
- Is there a brief but comprehensive "manning table" outlining your organizational structure and the key personnel you will need?
- Have your financial statements been provided in a reasonably detailed form?

Concerning the last item, your financial statements should include (1) a pro-forma income statement, showing the earnings impact of the financing being sought; (2) a pro-forma balance sheet, with a separate listing of those assets to be acquired by the requested financing; and (3) a projected monthly cash flow statement, showing the planned income and outgo for at least three years in the future.

The Deepest Pitfall of All

Without doubt, the most serious possible mistake you can make is to underestimate your initial financial needs. Keep in mind that the business may have several unprofitable years before it begins to show success. If you totally exhaust your finances before you get out of the red it could be fatal. Negotiating for more funds will be much more difficult the second time around, for several disadvantages will be encountered immediately.

First, any potential investor is likely to feel that you could be just as wrong calculating your money needs the second time as you were the first. Why should he have any confidence in your current estimate? Second, since you will be in a weak bargaining position, you will have to give up still more money to attract the additional venture capital. And third, if there can be any serious doubt as to your success, this is when it will emerge. The original investor will justifiably question whether he should get in any deeper, and a new investor may feel that he would be throwing good money after bad. In short, your proposal would be much more likely to encounter negative reactions from all sides.

The message is clear: plan so as to cut your expenses to the bone, eliminating all the frills from your project, and once you have done that be sure to allow for plenty of financing to see you through until profitability is achieved.

Protecting Your Interest During Negotiations

When and if your fishing expedition for money attracts a bite, you will need to spend as much effort checking out the potential venture capitalist as he will want to devote to investigating your offer. Among your prime concerns should be the following:

What kind of participation in your company does the venture capitalist expect for himself? (He may be able to help in various ways, but you should be the boss.)

What other business successes has the venture capitalist had? (Don't ask him; ask his employees or even some ex-employees.)

What kind of a financial record has the venture capitalist com-

piled? (It doesn't happen often, but once in a while you may be approached by an investor who has a very shady past. The time to find this out is *before* you take him into your company.)

How many outside contacts does the venture capitalist have and does he really have any leverage with them? (Remember, you have every right to expect your investor to channel some lucrative orders or accounts toward your business. Try to assess his potential influence with important people or customers.)

Do you think you will be personally compatible with the investor? (This is probably one of the most important considerations, as you will be seeing a lot of this fellow. It's best to be friends instead of simply tolerating each other.)

One last word of caution. It's likely that the intended venture capitalist will make a counterproposal to your initial offering. This is quite common; there's nothing improper about it. However, don't give in unless you feel that his offer is reasonable. In other words, don't be so pleased by the prospect of financial help that you sign away all of your own benefits. The negotiations for funding need not resemble the haggling of an oriental bazaar, but you should be prepared for some give and take. A successful venture must be profitable for *both* parties. Support your own position strongly so that the final agreement will preserve every possible advantage for *your* company.

Is Insurance-Company Financing a Viable Alternative?

Depending upon the nature of your business, it is sometimes possible to get financial support from an insurance company. Insurance companies are increasingly backing new business ventures. Chances are the industrial or commercial divisions of many medium-sized insurance companies are searching for someone just like you, so don't overlook this possible source of capital. However, you should understand that the money will be tendered in the form of a loan, which is somewhat different than the funding provided by a venture partner. The principal differences are as follows.

First, as indicated, an insurance loan agreement will be

drawn up instead of an agreement to share in the ownership of your company. Typically, no collateral need be supplied by your business; however, the lender will claim prior rights to your assets in the event the company is later liquidated. (These are about the same terms you can anticipate with any long-term loan from a financial institution.)

Second, there will normally be no participation in the management of your company on the part of an insurance representative. This may or may not be desirable, depending upon how much administrative or marketing help you feel you need. And third, an insurance-company loan will usually be for a 10- to 15-year term. This is long-range financing, in contrast with the shorter 5- to 7-year term which is the average length of most venture capitalists' involvement. The potential benefit for your company may be significant, since an insurance investor will not anticipate immediate profitability.

On first consideration, this type of financing may seem more acceptable to you than that of a venture capitalist. However, two drawbacks must be mentioned. In the first place, the availability of insurance investment money is limited—even more so than the normal flow of equity capital supplied by venture capitalists. As a result, the investigation conducted by an industrial or commercial representative of any insurance company is typically stringent and lengthy. In the second place, any loan made by an insurance investor is likely to be simply a long-term debt and nothing more. There is generally no management participation by the insurance company and little personal interest in the fate of your company. Instead, the emphasis is on your living up to the terms of the loan. The arrangement, then, is much more inflexible. If you have trouble meeting payment deadlines (and who hasn't encountered this situation from time to time?), then you must deal with but one more impatient creditor rather than with a sympathetic participant in your project, as a venture capitalist is likely to be. Worse, insurance-company financing could be hazardous: one or two missed payments could result in involuntary bankruptcy for you and dissolution of the business to satisfy your obligations. Thus, you should seriously consider the pros and cons before seeking financial help from an insurance investor.

Conclusion

As you know, the possibility of failure lurks behind every new business venture. Furthermore, the grander the new idea, the greater will be the impact if it flops. Thus, the burden on you and your business becomes greater as you aspire for more growth and more success. This chapter has presented a number of ideas for you to use in putting together an initial proposal for attracting outside financing. If you are successful in finding the money, that will only be the first hurdle: to develop a long-term, operationally sound business is also quite difficult, and to ensure continued, orderly growth and profitability is to face unending additional challenges.

However, consider the possible rewards. Back in the early 1900s, commercial radio was only a dream, and RCA was a struggling new venture; but look at it today. Henry Ford produced his first automobile in his own stable. The office photocopier, the electronic computer, and even television were once simply new ideas—until venture capital came into the picture. The list could be extended almost indefinitely. Who knows, possibly your product or service will be the latest addition.

It has been said that to decide to grow is the most dangerous decision a business manager can make. It can turn a small but thriving firm into one that's large but moribund. However, it is also the most lucrative business decision if the growth is properly managed. When you actively seek venture capital, you are choosing the rapid-expansion road. Once started, it will be up to you to administer your company properly, to keep it moving down that road toward profitability and success.

SECTION III

Your Fiscal Results Compared with Your Profit Plan

6

Using
Financial Statements
as Management Tools

A good way to break the ice when discussing something technical, such as the material contained in this chapter, is to tell a story. So, that's how we'll begin. This particular story happens to be true, although some details have been changed to protect confidentiality.

The main character of our story is an engineer who grew up in Latvia and came to the United States after World War II. He settled in Ohio and started his own business about a year and a half later. That business now produces and markets small mechanical assemblies, and though there are fewer than 50 employees in the company, gross sales exceed $1 million annually.

Every morning, our hero goes directly to the head bookkeeper as soon as he arrives at the plant. The bookkeeper always has a slip of paper ready with four figures on it, representing yesterday's totals of sales, factory costs, cash in bank, and outstanding receivables. Our businessman takes out a small black notebook from an inside coat pocket, copies the four amounts into it, and then methodically tears up the bookkeeper's slip of paper. He then moves directly to his private office, where he closes the door for about ten minutes. No one knows what he does during those ten minutes, but an educated guess is that he is making additional entries in the black notebook. In all probability, he calculates and enters several ratios or factors from the information provided by the bookkeeper.

In any case, he keeps the contents of that little book completely private. No one else has ever been allowed to see any of his entries. Furthermore, he *uses no other financial data* to run the business. He hardly ever looks at the yearly financial statements; he requests no special reports or statistics; he seldom asks the bookkeeper any questions.

During meetings or discussions with the staff, he takes out the little black book from time to time and glances at its contents. He may also do this when a capital expenditure is being considered (he approves all major expenditures), during a sales meeting, or in a conference about any sort of financial problem. The information in his black book obviously serves as a kind of "financial weathervane," pointing in the direction of a proper decision.

This story reveals a private and close-mouthed person who keeps his own counsel and reaches decisions alone. His use of the information entered in the black book compares to the way in which certain tools may be used to measure and predict the weather. Much like a farmer who plans his work day after going outdoors to test the wind and look at the sky, our businessman manages all of his financial affairs from those four daily bits of information.

Later in this chapter, we will have more to say about how you might also select appropriate "financial weathervanes." The purpose of this opening is to illustrate the principle. If the hero of our story can get along with a few basic figures, so can you. The trick is to know what data are important and how to use them.

This is a good example of *financial management by exception* (discussed in Chapter 2). In contrast with the company's bookkeeper, who must account for every penny received or spent, the owner of the business is interested chiefly in "vital signs" which indicate unusual occurrences—for instance, whether operating results are equal to expectations, whether there are individual cases of poor performance, if an unfavorable trend is developing, and so on. Periodic accounting statements will contain all of the pertinent information, but the indicators will either be buried among insignificant data or else reported too late for the owner to do much about the situation. That is why a daily review of selected data provides a better way to manage a small business financially.

How Financial Statements Are Derived

Although you are advised to use such sources of data very selectively, it is important to know a little about the manner in which financial statements are prepared. Every company uses these documents as the basis for calculating profits, paying taxes, or securing bank loans when necessary. Thus, you should have at least some familiarity with your accounting statements, since you will often be dealing with people who expect you to understand them. Figures 3 through 6 show the general format of these statements and also supply the totals used in explaining the technique of ratio analysis to be discussed shortly.

Your Business Balance Sheet

Think of your balance sheet as a "snapshot." It is a picture of what you own and what you owe, but the picture is accurate *only* on the morning of the day after your books are closed. By the end of the first business day of the new accounting period, various transactions will have occurred so that you will own and owe either more or less. With the passage of just a few more days, that original "snapshot" will be seriously out of focus! Thus, the time lag before you receive the balance sheet becomes very important. The longer you have to wait, the more out of date the information will be when you get it.

A typical balance sheet for a moderate-sized tool shop is illustrated in Figure 3. Note that this statement reveals the value and nature of the tool company's assets, as well as the size and character of its liabilities. Also indicated is the amount of the business owner's equity. However, you should understand that this latter information pertains only to the dollar value of the owner's equity, not to the cash fund or any other specific asset. In other words, it is impossible to "locate" an owner's investment among the various assets shown on the balance sheet, for it is likely to be split up among such things as buildings, land, factory equipment, cash, and so on.

Your Business Income Statement

In contrast to the "snapshot" presentation provided by your balance sheet, the business income statement tells a continuing story. In short, the income statement depicts the *accumulated results of your operations,* beginning with the first day of each new accounting period and continuing until the last day when the books are closed. This statement can be of particular interest to a potential investor or lender, since its bottom line shows the net profit earned during the entire period.

Continuing our example, the income statement for ABC Toolcraft Co. might look like Figure 4.

Because the cost of goods manufactured is substantial in our hypothetical case (about 40 percent of gross sales), the plant owner or manager might want to prepare a "cost of goods manufactured" statement in order to portray those costs in detail. Development of this statement would of course be optional. A typical report is depicted in Figure 5. In all probability, this sort of report would seldom be prepared by a small business, except one involved in some form of manufacturing or assembly.

Figure 3. ABC Toolcraft Co.—Balance sheet for the year ending June 30, 1978.

ASSETS

Current Assets

Cash		$ 5,000
Accounts receivable	$19,650	
Less allowance for uncollectibles	150	19,500
Inventories		
Finished goods	11,000	
Work in progress	2,500	
Raw materials	8,000	21,500
Tool room supplies		500
Prepaid insurance		900
Total Current Assets		$ 47,400

	Cost	*Less accumulated depreciation*	
Capital Assets			
Office equipment	1,700	700	1,000
Factory equipment	27,600	16,300	11,300
Building	52,500	11,000	41,500
Land	23,500	—	23,500

Total Assets	$124,700

LIABILITIES

Current Liabilities

Accounts payable	$ 3,800	
Income taxes (fed., state & local) due	1,500	
Salaries & wages payable	2,600	
Short-term loan payable	1,250	
Total Current Liabilities		$ 9,150
First mortgage on building— remainder due	40,000	
Total Liabilities		$ 49,150

STOCKHOLDER'S EQUITY

Common Stock, no par (1,000 shares auth. and issued)	50,000	
Retained Earnings	25,550	
Total Stockholders' Equity		75,550
Total Liabilities and Stockholders' Equity		$124,700

Figure 4. ABC Toolcraft Co.—Income statement for the year ending June 30, 1978.

Sales			$69,000
Cost of goods sold			
Finished-tools inventory, July 1, 1977	$ 3,500		
Cost of tools manufactured	33,500		
Total cost of tools available for sale		$37,000	
Less finished-tools inventory, June 30, 1978		11,000	
Cost of tools sold			26,000
Gross margin on sales			$43,000
Operating expenses			
Selling expenses			
Sales bonus	2,300		
Advertising expenses	400		
Miscellaneous selling expenses	500		
Total selling expenses		3,200	
General expenses			
Officer's salary	15,400		
Office salaries	17,575		
Depreciation—office equipment	700		
Bad debts, actual expense	150		
Miscellaneous office expenses	25		
Total general expenses		33,850	
Total operating expenses			37,050
Net income from operations			$ 5,950
Other expenses			
Interest expense			950
Net income before income taxes			$ 5,000
Income taxes (federal, state, and local)			1,500
Net income after income taxes			$ 3,500

Your Sources and Uses of Funds Statement

Although earned profit is the most important source of funds for any business, there are obviously other ways to get money. Extensive borrowing, for instance, is often utilized by a business with seasonal variations. In Figure 6, money ob-

Figure 5. ABC Toolcraft Co.—Cost of tools manufactured for the year ending June 30, 1978.

Work-in-progress inventory, July 1, 1977			$ 905
Raw materials			
Inventory, July 1, 1977	$5,700		
Purchases	5,200		
Cost of materials available for use		$10,900	
Less inventory, June 30, 1978		8,000	
Cost of material placed in production		2,900	
Direct labor		29,500	
Plant overhead costs			
Indirect labor	$ 250		
Factory maintenance	125		
Heat, light, and power	975		
Property taxes	270		
Depreciation, factory equipment	820		
Depreciation, building	80		
Factory supplies	75		
Insurance expense	75		
Miscellaneous production expense	25		
Total plant overhead		2,695	
Total manufacturing costs during period		35,095	
Total work in progress during period		36,000	
Less work-in-progress inventory, June 30, 1978		2,500	
Cost of tools manufactured		$33,500	

Figure 6. ABC Toolcraft Co.—Sources and uses of funds for the year ending June 30, 1978.

	June 30 1977	June 30 1978	Working Capital Sources	Working Capital Uses
Cash	$ 7,500	$ 5,000	$2,500	
Accounts receivable (net)	22,000	19,500	2,500	
All inventories	18,000	21,500		3,500
Prepaid expenses and supplies	600	1,400		800
Accounts payable	5,000	3,800		1,200
Income taxes due	1,200	1,500	300	
Salaries and wages payable	4,300	2,600		1,700
Short-term loan payable	50	1,250	1,200	
Total sources and uses			6,500	7,200
Decrease in working capital			700	
			$7,200	$7,200

Details of working-capital reduction

    Funds were supplied by:

Net profit (from income statement)	$3,500	
Add: Depreciation charged to operations	900	
Short-term loan	1,250	$5,650
Funds were applied to:		
Purchase of factory equipment	2,300	
Payments against mortgage on building	2,650	4,950
Decrease in working capital		$ 700

tained is listed in the "sources" column; money spent is entered under "uses."

These two kinds of information can be important for your *future* financial management. For example, next year's cash planning should be undertaken only after you know how much long- or short-term credit was used during the past year. As shown in Figure 6, the sources and uses of funds statement indicates new amounts borrowed and/or previous debts repaid for the previous period.

The "sources and uses of funds" report can also help a manager understand the impact of day-to-day financial decisions by summarizing the movement of financial resources in or out of the business and by documenting a net increase or decrease in working capital during the past accounting period.

Using Financial Ratio Analyses as Fiscal Weathervanes

Any single item included in one of your financial statements has but a limited meaning. It becomes much more significant when related to one or more other financial items. For instance, your cash on hand may look impressive until compared with the money needed to pay off your accounts payable. Or, your inventory may seem too high, except that your sales volume justifies the large stock. Most important, your net profit becomes really meaningful only in relation to the amount of capital that you have invested in the business.

The practice of ratio analysis has been developed to provide a business owner or investor with a systematic way of making various financial comparisons. In some cases, balance sheet totals are compared to each other. In others, income-statement entries are correlated. There are also a few instances where balance-sheet items are compared with income-statement items.

The method of relating these figures is very simple: one number is divided by the other. That is the reason for use of the mathematical term "ratio." The result can be multiplied by 100 and expressed as a percentage, or it can be expressed as a decimal figure without the percentage conversion step. You can easily make the calculations yourself by reference to your latest financial statements, and thus avoid any need to wait for your accountant or bookkeeper.

As you might imagine, the range of possible financial ratios is almost limitless. However, only a few are truly significant for the financial management of your small business. Proper understanding of these may point toward the beginning of a trend or highlight a significant deviation in your financial affairs. Whatever ratios you use, however, you should focus your attention on them only if they are out of the ordinary.

In case you feel that this subject has been mentioned before, you are correct; we are returning here to the topic of financial management by exception and the use of financial weathervanes. Indeed, the most important of the ratios which we will discuss below are called weathervane ratios. However, it would seem even more appropriate to borrow an analogy from physiology. Your body temperature, pulse, and blood pressure are all affected by the state of your health, but they can each signify different things to a physician. It is really a *combination* of various symptoms that enables the doctor to determine whether you have swine flu or an upset stomach. The same thing can be said about ratios derived from your business financial statements. Considered individually they don't necessarily signify anything; however, a series of ratios takes on a unique meaning when considered together. You can learn to diagnose the health of your business by reviewing some of them.

Testing for Liquidity

The ability to pay bills when they're due is one of the most vital of all signs of business health. This capability is referred to as *liquidity* and is best indicated by the *acid-test ratio,* or *quick ratio,* which is calculated as follows:

$$\frac{\text{Cash} + \text{marketable securities} + \text{accounts receivable}}{\text{Current liabilities}}$$

This ratio provides a stringent test of liquidity because it compares *only* those kinds of your current assets which are either cash or capable of being readily converted to cash against your total current liabilities. The current liabilities represent the most immediate need for cash, since they must be paid when due. Note that inventory, the asset which is generally considered to be least convertible-to-cash, is not included in this ratio. A conservative rule of thumb is that the acid-test ratio should never be less than 50 percent (or .5), although the kind of business, its size, and general practices in certain business fields may justify a slightly lower ratio. In any case, *this is a weathervane ratio.*

Testing for Solvency

The solvency of a business is somewhat different from its liquidity, as solvency has to do with the proper proportion of both current and long-term liabilities. Two ratios are considered to be significant solvency tests.

The *leverage ratio* indicates the extent to which borrowed money is used to obtain the assets of a business. It is calculated as follows:

$$\frac{\text{Total debt}}{\text{Total assets}}$$

This ratio illustrates a practice called "trading on the equity," which essentially refers to the practice of operating a profitable business while utilizing a high percentage of borrowed funds. Although the practice is considered risky by conservative financial analysts, it is a way to make more money than would be possible if only your "owner's equity" were to be used as a capital source. While this ratio is certainly a significant indicator of creditor confidence in a business, it is not considered to be a weathervane ratio.

The comparison of total business debts to total owners' equity (net worth) provides an even more important test for business solvency. It is calculated as follows:

$$\frac{\text{Total debt}}{\text{Total net worth}}$$

This ratio compares the amount of money *borrowed* for all purposes with the amount of money *invested* in the business by the owners. Generally, the more money borrowed compared to the money invested, the less solvent the business is. A conservative rule of thumb says that owner investment should provide at least two-thirds of the business's funds. Thus, to indicate satisfactory solvency, the ratio should be 66 percent (or .66) or less. *This is always a weathervane ratio.*

It is sometimes a trade practice to operate at a higher debt-to-net-worth ratio than the two-thirds maximum specified above. If that is the case in your industry, or if you are trading heavily "on the equity," the following supplemental ratio should also be computed:

$$\frac{\text{Total annual interest payments on debt}}{\text{Net profit before taxes}}$$

This ratio should always be less than 50 percent (or .5). The lower it is, the more solvent your company is. Since the need for calculating this ratio is irregular, it is not considered a weathervane ratio.

Testing for Sound Current Asset Management

Two categories of current assets require special attention because, if poorly managed, they can create a serious drain on your working capital. These are (a) all types of inventory, and (b) accounts receivable. To determine how well they are being managed, you can use ratios that measure the turnover for each asset category. *These are weathervane ratios,* and the methods of calculation are as follows:

$$\frac{\text{Cost of goods sold *}}{\text{Inventory (all types)}}$$

This ratio indicates how many times the inventory has been replaced (turned over) during the latest accounting period. You should always be interested in increasing inventory turnover, because each time inventory turns, more profit can be generated.

$$\frac{\text{Sales}}{\text{Accounts receivable}}$$

This ratio shows how many times your accounts receivable have been turned over (that is, paid off) during the latest

*Also called *cost of sales.*

accounting period. This is the first step in a two-step calculation intended to ensure that the level of accounts receivable
stays in reasonable proportion (see below for the second step).
Too many receivables outstanding will increase the likelihood
of excessive bad-debt losses. To determine the success of your
collection effort, make the following computation, using the
figure for accounts receivable turnover calculated in the first
step:

$$\frac{360}{\text{Accounts receivable turnover}}$$

This indicates the *average length of the collection period* for your
receivables; in other words, it shows how long your accounts
receivable are outstanding, on the average, before being paid.
For example, if your business carries accounts for a term of
30 days, and if the average collection period is calculated to be
45 or 60 days, your "past-due" (or collection follow-up) procedures are apparently not being carried out effectively.

Testing for Satisfactory Profitability

If your business has achieved a reasonable level of sales or
rentals, the first step has already been taken to reach a condition of satisfactory profitability. In financial circles, the annual
dollar volume of sales or rentals for any business is considered
an "opportunity for profit-making." Assuming that those
sales or rental dollars are being received by your company,
the question of the *degree of profitability* remains to be settled.
In the final anaysis, only you can decide if the business is
earning enough profit, because you alone know how much
money you want to make. (See the opening of Chapter 2 for a
discussion of your money-making goals.)

There are many ways to test for profitability. Four of the
most meaningful are discussed below. *All of them are weathervane ratios.*

The *profit-on-production* ratio is given by

$$\frac{\text{Gross margin}}{\text{Sales}}$$

where gross margin is defined as sales − cost of sales. This ratio measures the percentage of profit remaining after deducting the cost of buying or producing the goods or services being sold or rented by your company. It is an important indication of profit earned on production. However, it is incomplete since administrative and selling costs are not considered.

Another important ratio is the *return-on-sales* ratio:

$$\frac{\text{Net profit}}{\text{Sales}}$$

This ratio indicates the *profitability of the combined operation* of all phases of your business.

The *return-on-assets* ratio is calculated as

$$\frac{\text{Net profit}}{\text{Total assets}}$$

This ratio shows the profit earned on all assets employed in conducting the business. For any enterprise there is an appropriate level of required total assets. A tool shop needs more, for example, than does a lawyer's office. If there are too many assets in proportion to the dollar volume of sales, then the assets are being used inefficiently. If there are too few assets, the level of working capital is probably inadequate and a financial strain is being placed on the operation of your business.

Finally, a fourth, important ratio measuring profitability is the *return-on-equity* ratio:

$$\frac{\text{Net profit}}{\text{Net worth}}$$

This ratio measures the earnings that have been generated with the capital invested by all owners of the business. For that reason, it is sometimes referred to as the *return-on-investment* ratio. The ratio offers valuable guidance when a decision is to be made regarding the purchase of an expensive capital facility. It is also a helpful guide when additional overall investment in the business is under consideration. (Refer to Chapter 8 for further discussion of the return-on-investment concept.)

A Financial Analysis of the ABC Toolcraft Company

After plowing through a technical explanation of the various ratios, it would be useful to see a concrete example of their application. This is the best way to illustrate what you can accomplish by making similar calculations for your own business. So, let's go back to the balance sheet (Figure 3) and the income statement (Figure 4) of the ABC Toolcraft Company. All the data compiled for the firm in Figure 7 can be

Figure 7. ABC Toolcraft Co.—Financial-ratio analysis for the year ending June 30, 1978.

1. Acid test
$$\frac{\$5,000 + \$19,500}{\$9,150} = \frac{\$24,500}{\$9,150} = 2.68$$

2. Debt to net worth
$$\frac{\$49,150}{\$75,550} = 0.65$$

3. Inventory turnover
$$\frac{\$26,000}{\$21,500} = 1.21$$

4. Accounts receivable turnover
$$\frac{\$69,000}{\$19,500} = 3.54$$

$$\frac{360}{3.54} = 101.69 \text{ days}$$

5. Profit on production
$$\frac{\$43,000}{\$69,000} = 0.62$$

6. Return on sales
$$\frac{\$5,000}{\$69,000} = 0.073$$

7. Return on assets
$$\frac{\$5,000}{\$124,700} = 0.04$$

8. Return on equity
$$\frac{\$5,000}{\$75,500} = 0.066$$

traced back to those earlier two basic financial statements.

ABC's acid-test ratio of 2.68 is certainly very favorable. The firm has excellent liquidity as of June 30.

Its debt-to-net-worth ratio is .65, which is very close to the desired minimum of .66. Thus, its solvency, while by no means excellent, is reasonably satisfactory at present.

ABC's inventory turnover of 1.21 leaves something to be desired. However, a tool shop cannot expect to have the same rapid inventory turnover as a supermarket, because (a) the unit prices of its products are generally much higher, and (b) tool products are not such high-demand items as consumer goods.

ABC Toolcraft has done a really poor job on accounts receivable management during the past year. The calculated 102-day collection period signals the need for immediate attention. (Unfortunately, many small production plants, and tool shops in particular, have problems collecting past-due accounts.)

ABC's profit-on-production ratio is fairly good, since 62 cents out of every sales dollar is available to cover operating expenses, and a reasonable profit should also be possible.

The return on sales of ABC Toolcraft is .07 (or 7 percent) for the year. This is certainly not a fabulous rate of profitability, considering that the calculation was made using the annual net profit *before* income taxes. Whether or not the owner of this company is satisfied with 7 percent profitability will depend on his expectations as well as his desired standard of living. Note that "officer's salary" (under "general expenses" on the income statement) was $15,400 for the past year. Presumably, the owner either has another source of income or is keeping his salary low with the expectation of greater earnings sometime in the years ahead. In the latter case, he will surely have a future profitability goal of more than 7 percent.

ABC Toolcraft has a fairly substantial asset base. Its return on assets of .04 (or 4 percent), is less than two-thirds of what could be earned if the same money had been invested in certificates of deposit for the last twelve months. Few investors would be satisfied with such a result.

Finally, its return on equity of .066 (or roughly 7 percent) is only moderately satisfactory.

Since the final three profitability ratios are all on the low side, more attention should be paid to the level of annual operating expenses. If these could be cut, profits would rise considerably.

The various considerations discussed above should give you an idea of the conclusions which can be drawn if the financial statements of your own company are subjected to a similar anaysis. Why not give it a try?

How to Make Ratio Analysis More Meaningful

Suppose your newsboy delivered the daily paper only on the first day of each month, or, worse still, only on the first day of each new year. Do you think you could keep abreast of local, national, or world affairs by reading a newspaper once a year or even once a month? Of course not. On the other hand, how often do you see fresh financial statements for your business? Very likely you see them once a year, or certainly no more than once a month, and at that rate even your weathervane ratios can only describe fairly ancient history, since they have been derived from accounting totals far out of date.

However, there's a remedy that you can take. Go back to the story at the beginning of this chapter, the one about the small businessman and his little black book. Now that you know a little more about financial statements, you may rightly conclude that the entries in that black book are simply updates of some important balance-sheet and income-statement data. It is probable that the businessman in our story has a select set of weathervane ratios, which he recalculates every day. But, in order to stay current, he first *recomputes a new balance for* (1) cash on hand, (2) accounts receivable outstanding, (3) sales to date, and (4) factory costs to date.

Get the point? You can keep track of some of the most vital aspects of your business's financial performance by devoting just ten minutes a day to this chore. As a part of that ten minutes, you should calculate an approximate current version of at least three weathervane ratios: acid test, accounts receivable turnover, and profit on production. Why not try this for a month? (Be sure to start immediately after receiving the latest set of financial statements.) You may be so pleased to have more current information that you'll never give it up!

Conclusion

Many small business managers find it worthwhile to occasionally compare their financial situation with that of the average in their industry, as well as with past performances of their own company. Such comparisons can provide a measure of operating efficiency and will also indicate competitive strength. A number of trade associations collect this data and regularly supply comparative ratio information to their membership. Dun & Bradstreet, Inc., publishes a series of ratios for more than 70 business lines, and Robert Morris Associates furnishes statement studies for over 300 types of companies.

The use of comparisons such as these will help you measure business achievements against objectives. The various ratios provide a reasonable (if somewhat dated) way to gauge how well your equity capital, and capital derived by borrowing, has been used. Financial ratios can also provide various indications of your business success or show that something may be going wrong. This will be especially true if the results of these ratios can be measured against your company objectives.

All business goals should be set with the expectation of achieving them, but of course such achievement remains only a possibility until the final financial results are in. However, by using the ratios discussed in this chapter as "signposts," you will be able to obtain a much clearer picture of the direction your business is taking. This will be particularly true if you concentrate on the weathervane ratios, and also if you follow the recommended practice of updating them with current accounting data.

7

The Benefits of a Breakeven Analysis for Your Business

IT goes without saying that the sales or rental volume of your business is extremely important. No matter how much profitability is "built into" the individual prices of your product or service—that is, no matter how much of a spread there is between individual total costs and unit prices—there can be no profit earned unless the accumulation of sales or rentals is great enough. For this reason, you no doubt have often wondered how high your business income must be before you start to make money each month. Or perhaps you have already estimated a certain dollar amount above which profit-making should begin. In either case, this chapter is designed to help you. In the former case, you will be able to compute your breakeven point for the first time, and in the latter case you'll be able to verify (and possibly adjust) the breakeven estimate you had previously made.

Where profitability begins is vital; it should have an important influence on the way in which you manage the business. The planning you do and the decisions you make when the business is operating at a profit are likely to be different from those made when the business is in the red. When you are able to spend money without wondering if current income will cover the expense, when you can determine the present profit or loss status from an up-to-date report of sales or rentals; then you truly have a finger on the fiscal pulse of your business.

The "Direct Costing" Concept

The idea of cost analysis was introduced in Chapter 2 in a discussion on preparing a budget. It may be helpful here to go back over that material, since the two most important cost concepts used in breakeven analysis were outlined in connection with budgeting. In Chapter 2 the term *variable cost* was used to refer to those expense items that increase or decrease as your business expands or contracts and which are *directly* related to the output of your goods or services. In the same chapter, we also discussed *fixed costs,* which, by definition, remain constant no matter how much or how little you sell or rent. Now it is time to say a little more about those two cost categories.

First of all, consider your fixed costs. These are generally the kinds of expenses which the business incurs from day to day, based on earlier plans regarding your method of operation and the kinds of products or services you chose to deal in. In other words, the fixed costs are usually the result of pre-established decisions, and as such, they are relatively inflexible. These costs are also associated with employees or facilities which your business keeps either "in readiness" or "in action," but which cost the same regardless of their status. (Other terms that are used by accountants to describe such expenses are *committed costs* and *overhead costs.*) By their nature, costs of this type will almost automatically be reincurred during every future accounting period, *unless you take specific steps to discontinue them.* This is important to keep in mind; we'll come back to it later.

With reference to the variable costs of your business, there is a danger of oversimplification. Remember the Chapter 2 definition: "Variable costs are those which are directly related to output and which vary with that output." Strictly speaking, then, the only real direct costs of a business are raw materials, production labor, and production supplies. However, this interpretation actually is overly strict; many kinds of costs other than production expenses vary with output and are associated directly with a product or service. Delivery expense is an example; so are costs connected with equipment maintenance, janitor service, long-distance telephone calls, salesmen's commissions, and so on. In short, *variable costs are all those business expenses which are undertaken to promote the sales or rentals of a specific product or service line, and which always fluctuate directly with the volume of sales or rentals.*

The separation of your business costs into fixed and variable costs is sometimes referred to as the *direct costing* concept. It offers the following important advantages:

- It permits assignment of responsibility for profits or losses, both insofar as your employees are concerned and also with respect to specific products or services. That is because each separate variable cost has an impact on profit. Every contributor to variable cost influences profit *negatively,* and each variable cost cutter affects profit *positively.*

- The direct costing concept provides better control of the overhead of your business by allowing you to identify fixed costs and to consider them separately. Your bookkeeper should never "spread" these fixed costs across the products or services provided by your business. Your cost control is diluted when the record-keeping mixes variable and fixed costs by allocating some of each to the various products or services you provide.

- Separation of business costs into either fixed or variable categories permits direct computation of a dollar amount which is your breakeven sales or rental total. It also provides the basis for a graphical representation of breakeven dollars. We will spend the remainder of the chapter discussing the financial management aspects of these very useful analytical tools.

The Uses of Financial Breakeven Analysis

As you might suppose, the breakeven point refers to that volume where the money received for total sales or rentals equals the total costs. From the viewpoint of your business, this is a crucial stage; you have neither made nor lost money but all of your costs for the period will be covered. After determining where you break even, this chapter will show how to get reasonably correct answers to such questions as

- If you change selling price, what happens to profits?
- If you reduce costs or expenses, how much more profit will you earn?
- At a given sales volume, what will the profit be?
- If you intend to earn a certain dollar profit, how much will you have to sell or rent to achieve your goal?
- What will happen to profit if you:
    Hire another employee?
    Start using cheaper raw materials?
    Buy a more efficient machine?
    Discharge a key official?
    Grant a general wage increase?

Think of the managerial implications of being able to answer such questions! Remember, however, that determination of the breakeven point will be only approximately accurate, because it will be based on financial information developed at the end of the previous accounting period. (Why accounting figures rapidly become obsolete was explained in Chapter 6.) Given the built-in inaccuracies, the breakeven analysis method cannot provide absolutely exact results. Its utility might be compared to that of a yardstick: it is crude, but accurate enough for most of the measuring you do around the house. Similarly, the breakeven point is reliable enough for most of your financial management decision making.

Direct Calculation of Breakeven Sales or Rentals

Now, let's turn to the methods by which you and your bookkeeper can determine the breakeven point. The first approach to be explained is the *direct calculation* procedure. This is the easiest method and has the most managerial applications. The following formula yields the dollar amount of your sales or rental breakeven:

$$\text{Breakeven point} = \frac{\text{fixed cost total}}{100\% - \left(\frac{\text{total variable cost} \times 100}{\text{total sales or rentals}}\right)}$$

A simpler way to express the same formula is as follows:

$$\text{Breakeven point} = \frac{\text{fixed cost total}}{100\% - \text{variable cost as a \% of sales}}$$

One way to clarify the use of this formula for your bookkeeper is to go back to the financial statements of ABC Toolcraft in Chapter 6. A hypothetical breakdown of fixed and variable expenses, taken from ABC's income statement and its "cost of tools manufactured" analysis is shown in Figure 8.

In reviewing Figure 8, bear two things in mind. First, quite a few of the cost categories are covered under both the "fixed" and the "variable" columns. Such costs are semifixed and semivariable, which means that some of the transactions included in a particular category were not related to the output, while others were. Obviously, that part of the cost which was related was included in the "variable" column; that part which was not related was put in the "fixed" column. A great many of the costs your business incurs will be similarly divided— which is why your bookkeeper should help prepare this analysis. He or she will be able to calculate how costs should be split, if appropriate.

The second thing to keep in mind with respect to Figure 8 is that ABC Toolcraft would have incurred $36,330 in fixed expenses for the year *regardless of the amount of tool sales made.* Also, for every dollar of sales for the year, the variable (that is, direct) cost amounted to 52.5 cents.

We now have enough information to calculate the yearly breakeven sales point for ABC Toolcraft.

Figure 8. ABC Toolcraft Co.—Fixed- and variable-cost analysis for the year ending June 30, 1978.

Description	Amt. of Fixed Cost	Amt. of Variable Cost	Variable Cost as a % of $69,000 Sales
Raw material placed in production	—	$ 2,900	4.0%
Direct labor	—	29,500	43.0%
Indirect labor	$ 130	120	0.2%
Factory maintenance	65	60	0.1%
Heat, light, and power	550	425	1.0%
Property taxes	270	—	—
Depreciation, factory equipment	820	—	—
Depreciation, buildings	80	—	—
Factory supplies expenses	25	50 ⎫	
Insurance expenses	75	— ⎬ 0.1%	
Miscellaneous production expenses	5	20 ⎭	
Sales bonus	—	2,300	3.0%
Advertising expenses	25	375	1.0%
Miscellaneous selling expenses	435	65	0.1%
Officer's salary	15,400	—	—
Office salaries	17,575	—	—
Depreciation, office equipment	700	—	—
Bad-debts expenses	150	—	—
Miscellaneous office expenses	25	—	—
Totals	$36,330	$35,815	52.5%

$$\text{Breakeven point} = \frac{\$36,330}{100\% - 52.5\%}$$

$$= \frac{\$36,330}{47.5\%} \quad \text{or} \quad \frac{\$36,330}{.475}$$

$$= \$76,484$$

Considering that this company enjoyed only $69,000 in sales for the year (see Figure 4 in Chapter 6), it is apparent that it is in a loss position. It could temporarily become profitable by retaining a considerable amount of its finished tools as unsold finished inventory, and in fact, a glance at Figure 4 tells you that that's what was done. ABC's beginning finished-tool inventory was $3,500, while its ending finished-tool inventory was $11,000. If much of that $11,000 had been sold, the company would have lost money for the year. Its income statement does show a small net profit ($3,500) after taxes, but the company has a potential loss coming up unless it can substantially increase sales or cut down on expense somewhere.

You can see how valuable a knowledge of the breakeven point would have been during the past year to the management of ABC Toolcraft. Furthermore, an examination of the percentages in its fixed and variable cost analysis (Figure 8) gives a clue as to one source of the trouble. The direct labor costs are 43 percent of sales! It's apparent that a reduction here would provide a solution to ABC's lack of profitability.

There is a three-way relationship between fixed cost, variable cost, and sales that should be understood by every small-business owner or manager; it's important at all times, and can be crucial in a situation such as that which ABC Toolcraft is facing. Suppose you were the owner of this company. Obviously, some remedial action is needed to create profitability. One question that might occur to you in this situation is how many more dollars in sales would the business need in order to earn such and such a profit? If you knew the answer, you would at least have a sales target to shoot for.

We can utilize the breakeven formula to answer that question, assuming that a reasonable growth in sales would not significantly distort the cost percentages that we've already calculated. The formula would now look like this:

$$\text{Increased sales target} = \frac{\text{fixed cost total} + \text{desired net profit}}{100\% - \text{variable cost as a \% of sales}}$$

Let's use $10,000 as the desired net profit. The calculation for ABC Toolcraft would then be as follows:

$$\text{Increased sales target} = \frac{\$36,330 + \$10,000}{100\% - 52.5}$$

$$= \frac{\$46,330}{47.5\%} \quad \text{or} \quad \frac{\$46,330}{.475}$$

$$= \$97,537$$

Another solution you could try is to reduce the business fixed cost, rather than increase sales or cut back on direct labor. In such a case, the breakeven formula would be changed as follows:

Modified breakeven point

$$= \frac{\text{original fixed cost total} - \text{fixed cost reduction}}{100\% - \text{variable cost as a \% of sales}}$$

Let's say that you've decided to reduce the office staff by discharging an employee who earns $9,750 a year. The new breakeven calculation for ABC Toolcraft would then be:

$$\text{Modified breakeven point} = \frac{\$36,330 - \$9,750}{100\% - 52.5\%}$$

$$= \frac{\$26,580}{47.5\%} \quad \text{or} \quad \frac{\$26,580}{.475}$$

$$= \$55,958$$

Isn't that interesting? Notice what an impact a reduction of fixed cost has on the breakeven point. This should provide considerable food for thought for you. Remember the statement made earlier in this chapter, that fixed costs will continually be reincurred, unless you do something to reduce them. Now do you see what a fixed cost reduction can mean?

As we've seen in this example, it is also often beneficial to reduce variable costs. Unfortunately, it may be difficult to do so unless there is some kind of technological breakthrough that dramatically changes the way the goods or services are produced. Suppose, for example, that a new kind of material became available to ABC Toolcraft—say, a machinable plastic—that could be substituted for many uses of steel and which costs much less to handle. If you could lower the "direct labor" expense in Figure 8 from $29,500 to $25,000 by using the plastic, it would automatically lower the variable cost as a percentage of sales from 52.5 percent to 45.5 percent. As a result, the new breakeven calculation for ABC Toolcraft would be as follows:

$$\text{Modified breakeven point} = \frac{\$36,330}{100\% - 45.5\%}$$

$$= \frac{\$36,330}{54.5\%} \quad \text{or} \quad \frac{\$36,330}{.545}$$

$$= \$66,661$$

It should be obvious by now that the breakeven formula provides a useful analysis for your business. It may be troublesome for your bookkeeper to divide the costs of your company into fixed and variable, but it really is worth the effort. There are, furthermore, other kinds of calculations you can perform once you know zhe total fixed cost and the variable cost percentages. For instance, the following formula simply represents common sense:

Total sales or rentals = fixed cost + variable cost + operating profit

With this formula, you can either start with an arbitrarily selected amount of operating profit and (given the two types of cost) calculate the sales total needed to achieve that profit, or you can turn it around and calculate the operating profit that would be derived from a preestablished sales total. Let's do the latter for ABC Toolcraft, using $75,000 as the selected sales target:

$$\$75,000 = \$36,330 + (\$75,000 \times 52.5\%) + \text{operating profit}$$
$$= \$36,330 + \$39,375 + \text{operating profit}$$
$$= \$75,705 + \text{operating profit}$$

Operating profit = $- \$705$ (loss)

These examples have shown some of the ways that your managerial decision making might be improved by straightforward calculation of the breakeven point for your small business. However, other decisions might be easier to make with the help of a graphic presentation of breakeven. Let's move on to explore that subject.

Graphic Presentation of Breakeven Sales or Rentals

Referring back to our definitions of fixed and variable costs, remember that the former are those which always remain constant, no matter how much or how little is sold or rented. If we apply that definition to our ABC Toolcraft, its yearly fixed cost would be graphed as the horizontal line shown in Figure 9.

Now, let's add a line to the chart to depict ABC's yearly sales. (To simplify the procedure, we'll assume that sales grew at a relatively constant rate all year, which means that its sales line will be straight.) The composite will now appear as shown

Figure 9. ABC Toolcraft Co.—Fixed costs for the year ending June 30, 1978.

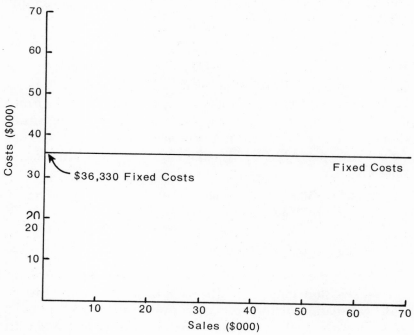

in Figure 10. Note that the point representing total sales of $69,000 is located on both the horizontal and vertical axes of the graph (that is, on both the sales and cost sides of the graph). This is necessary to permit indication of variable cost as a proportion of sales in the analysis that follows.

Now that sales and fixed costs for ABC Toolcraft are both represented on the graph, we are ready to add a line for variable costs. These costs, remember, are those that are directly related to output (the more output, the greater the variable cost). To show variable cost graphically in accordance with this definition, we want a straight line that rises gradually as it moves from left to right. The question is, where should the line be drawn?

Since variable costs are incurred over and above fixed costs, the low point of the variable-cost line should be just above the horizontal fixed-cost line on the graph, while the

Figure 10. ABC Toolcraft Co.—Fixed costs and sales for the year ending June 30, 1978.

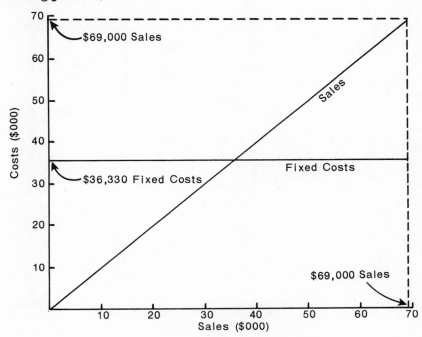

high point should be set at the proper percent of sales. However, since it will be more meaningful to you if ABC Toolcraft
is a profitable company, we will now change the example a bit.
We'll reduce direct labor cost from $29,500 to $25,000 on the
assumption that ABC has been able to get its hands on some
of that machine plastic. Thus, the high point of the variable-
cost line will now be at 45.5 percent of sales. The result is
shown in Figure 11.

Notice that the variable-cost line crosses the sales line close
to the upper right corner of the graph. *The point where it crosses
is the new breakeven point.* It is located on the graph at about
$66,000. This is close to the $66,661 which we had previously
calculated for ABC Toolcraft after arbitrarily reducing its
direct labor cost from $29,500 to $25,000. (The slight difference between the calculated and the graphically derived
breakeven points is the result of the imprecision which is al-

**Figure 11. ABC Toolcraft Co.—Sales breakeven for the year ending
June 30, 1978.**

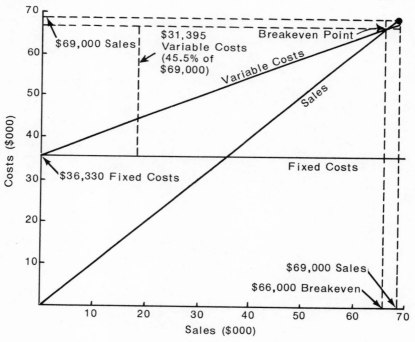

ways experienced when plotting a chart, as opposed to per-
forming an arithmetic computation.)

You will find that a breakeven chart will often be useful
because it supplies a visual picture of the interrelationship
between the two cost categories and total sales or rentals.
Thus, you can better understand how a change in one will
influence the others. Let's consider, for instance, how such a
chart could help you prepare for an anticipated slump in sales
in your own company.

Figure 12 illustrates the substantial ameliorating effect a
moderate reduction in fixed cost would have in the event of a
sales decline. In the example shown in the figure, fixed costs

Figure 12. Breakeven point lowered by reducing fixed costs.

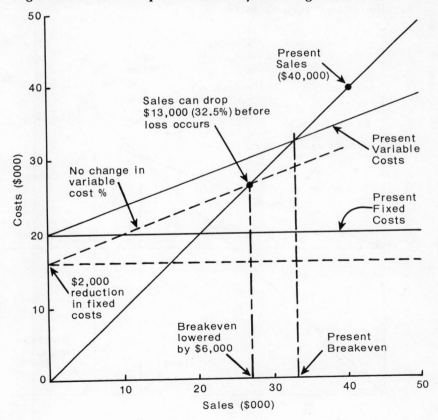

were cut by $2,000, or 10 percent. As a result, the level of sales could diminish almost one-third before a net loss would result. That could be very useful information to have when sales are dropping, since it would provide quite a cost-reduction incentive.

Taking another example, suppose that a new and larger machine tool is being considered for the business in Figure 12. Because of the increased size, a larger output would be possible, and variable production costs would therefore be reduced by 5 percent. However, an increase in depreciation expense would also be incurred, thus adding to the fixed cost. Figure 13 shows the breakeven graph for this example. Such

Figure 13. Breakeven point raised due to increased fixed costs, despite reduced variable costs.

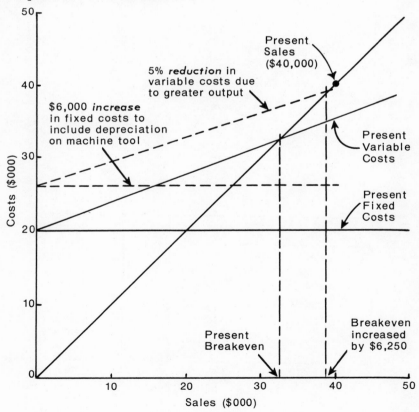

a graph should make it fairly easy to reach a decision to buy or not to buy. And in the case of the machine tool, the decision should be negative, since the breakeven point would increase so much that it would be almost equal to the present level of sales.

The range of situations where a breakeven chart is useful will vary according to the kind and size of a business. But no matter what sort of company you are operating, you can make some use of this valuable visual tool. The possibilities are limited only by your interest, your ingenuity, and your understanding of the technique.

Conclusion

This chapter has had two primary aims: to illustrate how the concept of breakeven analysis can help answer many of your financial management questions, and to expand your understanding of the use of mathematics for business decision making. When you stop to think about it, any important decision regarding your business should satisfy *all* of the following criteria: it should be (1) possible to accomplish, (2) advantageous to the business, (3) legally permissible, and (4) profitable.

There are many intangible considerations which could influence your choices with respect to the first three qualities, but the last requirement is clear-cut: income must always exceed outgo. And this is where arithmetic computation is most helpful.

With most business problems, the difficulty is to find out in advance if your solution will create profitability. By utilizing mathematical techniques such as those explained in this chapter, you'll be as close as is humanly possible to a sound business solution. You can never obtain an absolutely infallible answer, due to out-of-date accounting information and because there are so many unknowns. However, you will be accurate enough to minimize the risk. In a nutshell, that's the main benefit of breakeven analysis for your business.

8

Estimating
the Return on
Your Investment
in Capital Assets

IT is the rare business that is not frequently offered an opportunity to spend money on new capital facilities. Interesting proposals are constantly being presented by some salesman promoting his product line. Almost as frequently the manager of the business or a key subordinate may mull over such possibilities as: Should we expand the size of the operation? Do we need to invest in more machinery? Should we add another product to complement our present line? Should we modernize some of the older equipment?

Does this list sound familiar? It should, if you intend your business to grow. Decisions made today regarding capital expenditures will help create a foundation for tomorrow's business development and can affect the competitive position of your company for years to come. In short, a series of good capital investments will carry any company a long way down the road toward profitability and success, while a few poor investments can have an equally great, negative influence. Thus, this chapter will deal with one of the key questions in the realm of financial management—whether or not to acquire specific capital equipment, or once a decision to spend money is made, how to tell which capital acquisition is best for the company.

Let's begin with some definitions. These will make clear what we are talking about.

Capital asset. You should already be acquainted with the term *asset,* which simply refers to anything of value that is owned and used by a business. A capital asset is any asset which is worth more than a certain arbitrary amount (let's set $100 as a useful base for reference) and which will not be worn out or rendered obsolete within a specific time span (let's say one year, again for the sake of uniformity).

This definition isn't quite complete, however, since under the above terms, a tank of heating oil might be considered to be a capital asset, as it would be worth several hundred dollars and could conceivably keep the shop warm for more than one winter. However, the heating oil is more realistically classified as a supply item, thus placing it outside the scope of this chapter. Our definition, then, must have to do with the *nature* of various business assets. Typically, a list of capital assets owned by a company would include buildings, machines, cars and trucks, office equipment, display cases, and so on. As you can see, we're talking about durable items that are important to the business, have a high unit cost, and last a long time.

Return on investment (ROI). This term was mentioned in Chapter 6, in connection with ratio analysis. However, whereas in Chapter 6 we were interested in the ROI for the entire business, our concern now is with the ROI of particular capital assets. Expressed as a simple arithmetic formula, the ROI calculation for a capital asset looks like this:

$$\text{Asset ROI} = \frac{\text{average contribution to profit}}{\text{amount of investment}}$$

As an example, let's determine the ROI for a new accounting machine.

Cost of the new machine . . . $7,500
Annual clerical savings
estimated to be generated
by the machine $3,750

$$\text{Asset ROI} = \frac{\$3,750}{\$7,500} = .5 \times 100\% = 50\%$$

Capital asset profitability. This term simply refers to the potential for earning money (or cutting costs) that various capital assets offer. As with asset ROI, the rate of asset profitability is usually expressed as a percentage. However, asset profitability is not synonymous with ROI, because a time factor is involved. For instance, when comparing the virtues of two or more capital assets, we would first ask what the respective ROI rate would be for each asset (in other words, what each would contribute to profit), and then we would want to know how long it would take for each asset to contribute that much.

To cite an example, if the accounting machine discussed in the previous illustration were expected to last five years, its annual profit contribution would obviously be 10 percent, using the formula

$$\frac{\text{Total asset ROI}}{\text{Estimated life of asset in years}}$$

Time value of money. One of the truisms of financial management is that a dollar earned today is more valuable than a dollar that will be earned sometime in the future. That's because of the income that today's dollar can generate in the interval before a future dollar is received. Conversely, a dollar that must be paid out today is more burdensome than a dollar the company is obligated to pay at a later date. This is due to the income which must be given up in the meantime. Table 3 shows a simplified example that illustrates the time value of money.

Table 3. The time value of a dollar.

Year n	How $1.00 invested at 15% compound interest will grow in value	What $1.00 to be received in Year n is worth today at a discount rate of 15%
The present	$1.00	$1.00
1 year from today	1.15	0.87
2 years from today	1.32	0.76
3 years from today	1.52	0.66
4 years from today	1.74	0.57
5 years from today	2.01	0.50

Note: 15% may seem an unusually high rate, and it would be if you were borrowing money; but it is not at all unusual for the ROI of a valuable asset to *exceed* 15%.

We have already discussed the importance of cash planning for the future from the small-business standpoint. When trying to decide whether or not to spend money on a capital asset, we must keep in mind its potential annual profitability, as well as its immediate cost (what earning potential must be given up when the price of the asset is paid out in cash). The arithmetic process for evaluating these considerations in combination will be discussed in the next two sections of this chapter. Also, we will show how to compare and rank the desirability of spending money on either of two completely different capital assets, such as a truck or a set of showcases. The mathematical techniques involved are still comparatively unknown to the small-business community, where decisions to spend large sums are more frequently influenced by the difficulty of obtaining the money than by any calculated effect on profitability.

Payback Evaluation

Certainly the simplest way to decide if a capital asset should be purchased is to determine how much time will be needed to recover its cost. This approach is called the *payback* (or *payout*) method. In calculating payback, we do not take the time value of money into account. Instead, payback simply shows the so-called financial-risk factor of investing in any particular capital asset. Under this method, *the longer the payback, the greater the risk.* Since a business is unlikely to obtain a new capital asset just to get the money back later, any payback calculation should also include a long-range deter-mination of the total ROI likely to be earned by that asset. However, sometimes the payback and total asset ROI results are confusing when several different assets are being con-sidered for purchase.

Table 4. Payback evaluation for two alternative capital assets.

Year	ROI Contribution of Asset A (Initial Cost = $10,000)	ROI Contribution of Asset B (Initial Cost = $12,500)
1	$2,500	$1,000
2	2,500	1,500
3	2,000	1,500
4	1,750	2,000
5	1,250 *	2,000
6	1,000	2,500
7	1,000	2,000 *
8	—	1,000
9	—	1,000
10	—	1,000
Total contribution	$12,000	$15,500

* Investment paid back during that year.

Table 4 shows how total payback is influenced by time and initial investment. Asset A pays back its cost in five years, while asset B takes seven years. Notice, however, that the *total* contribution of B exceeds A by $3,500, and the long-range profitability percentage for B is 129 percent compared to 120 percent for A (computed by the asset ROI formula). But, again, B's contribution takes ten years to be fully earned, while A's is earned in but seven years.

Here, we have a typical dilemma. Different aspects of the calculation indicate different priorities. The reason is that (as stated above) the payback method doesn't take the time value of money into consideration. In short, we can't accurately rank the desirability of buying either asset A or asset B using this method.

Discounted Cash-Flow Evaluation

In order to really determine whether asset A or asset B will prove to be the most profitable, we must use a more complex approach. But before getting into details, let's pause to consider why the extra complexity is justified.

Your business will need to be selective in deciding when and where to invest in capital assets any time that the following two conditions prevail: (1) when there is need for a variety of capital assets; and (2) when there is not an unlimited supply of money to spend for these assets. The need to spend money can originate at about the same time in several different areas of the business, and it can result from various competitive pressures or from the existence of several alternative opportunities to increase earnings. No matter what the reason, you are likely to face many difficult acquisition decisions of this sort in the course of managing the business. There will be strong pressure to spend more money than can be spared, or more than can prudently be borrowed. If you have ever had to make a choice between two or more such needs or opportunities, you can appreciate the problem. Your final decision should rest largely on which of the several assets will create the most profitability, and that's what the discounted cash-flow (or present value) method can best tell you.

This computation requires that a series of trial calculations be made. The ROI for a particular asset under consideration must be discounted at various percentages until one of the net present-value calculations proves to be as close to zero as possible. Using that ROI percentage as a "starter," we then make another present-value calculation at an interest rate either a few percentage points higher (if the result of the starter calculation was slightly more than zero) or a few percentage points lower (if the result of the starter calculation was slightly less than zero).

As a final step, we interpolate to determine the exact ROI for that asset. This is repeated for each of the various other assets also being considered for acquisition. The asset offering the highest exact ROI should be selected if the rate of return is attractive and if there is only enough money to permit one asset to be purchased. If enough funds are available to purchase additional assets, the selections should be made in descending ROI sequence. This will ensure the greatest return for your money. (If you have difficulty understanding this explanation of the computation, don't be surprised or embarrassed. This is perhaps the most complicated of all the calculations in this book. And yet, if you just follow the format provided, it can be reasonably simple to use.)

One of the most important ways of simplifying this calculation is to use the data in Table 5, which shows precalculated present values. From this table you can find the present value of $1 received *n* years from today, at various discount rates. To use this table in estimating the time value of ROI (that is, real ROI), select the ROI you would hope that an asset would earn in a given year, and multiply that amount by the corresponding factor from the table. You will derive the present value of the estimated ROI for that future year. Finally, by adding together all the ROI present values for each of the years that the asset is expected to be useful, you can determine what the entire income stream anticipated to be produced in the future by that asset is worth *right now*—in other words, you establish its total net ROI present value.

Let's work a discounted cash-flow example (see Table 6). Suppose that you operate a pizzeria supply company. Asset A could be a high volume dough mixer costing $10,000, with a life of seven years and a gradually declining ROI contribution. Let's assume it has no salvage value at the end of year

Table 5. Present value of $1 received *n* years hence, at different discount rates.

Years Hence	1%	2%	4%	6%	8%	10%	12%	14%	15%	16%	18%	20%	22%	24%	25%	26%	28%	30%	35%	40%	45%	50%
1	0.990	0.980	0.962	0.943	0.926	0.909	0.893	0.877	0.870	0.862	0.847	0.833	0.820	0.806	0.800	0.794	0.781	0.769	0.741	0.714	0.690	0.667
2	0.980	0.961	0.925	0.890	0.857	0.826	0.797	0.769	0.756	0.743	0.718	0.694	0.672	0.650	0.640	0.630	0.610	0.592	0.549	0.510	0.476	0.444
3	0.971	0.942	0.889	0.840	0.794	0.751	0.712	0.675	0.658	0.641	0.609	0.579	0.551	0.524	0.512	0.500	0.477	0.455	0.406	0.364	0.328	0.296
4	0.961	0.924	0.855	0.792	0.735	0.683	0.636	0.592	0.572	0.552	0.516	0.482	0.451	0.423	0.410	0.397	0.373	0.350	0.301	0.260	0.226	0.198
5	0.951	0.906	0.822	0.747	0.681	0.621	0.567	0.519	0.497	0.476	0.437	0.402	0.370	0.341	0.328	0.315	0.291	0.269	0.223	0.186	0.156	0.132
6	0.942	0.888	0.790	0.705	0.630	0.564	0.507	0.456	0.432	0.410	0.370	0.335	0.303	0.275	0.262	0.250	0.227	0.207	0.165	0.133	0.108	0.088
7	0.933	0.871	0.760	0.665	0.583	0.513	0.452	0.400	0.376	0.354	0.314	0.279	0.249	0.222	0.210	0.198	0.178	0.159	0.122	0.095	0.074	0.059
8	0.923	0.853	0.731	0.627	0.540	0.467	0.404	0.351	0.327	0.305	0.266	0.233	0.204	0.179	0.168	0.157	0.139	0.123	0.091	0.068	0.051	0.039
9	0.914	0.837	0.703	0.592	0.500	0.424	0.361	0.308	0.284	0.263	0.225	0.194	0.167	0.144	0.134	0.125	0.108	0.094	0.067	0.048	0.035	0.026
10	0.905	0.820	0.676	0.558	0.463	0.386	0.322	0.270	0.247	0.227	0.191	0.162	0.137	0.116	0.107	0.099	0.085	0.073	0.050	0.035	0.024	0.017
11	0.896	0.804	0.650	0.527	0.429	0.350	0.287	0.237	0.215	0.195	0.162	0.135	0.112	0.094	0.086	0.079	0.066	0.056	0.037	0.025	0.017	0.012
12	0.887	0.788	0.625	0.497	0.397	0.319	0.257	0.208	0.187	0.168	0.137	0.112	0.092	0.076	0.069	0.062	0.052	0.043	0.027	0.018	0.012	0.008
13	0.879	0.773	0.601	0.469	0.368	0.290	0.229	0.182	0.163	0.145	0.116	0.093	0.075	0.061	0.055	0.050	0.040	0.033	0.020	0.013	0.008	0.005
14	0.870	0.758	0.577	0.442	0.340	0.263	0.205	0.160	0.141	0.125	0.099	0.078	0.062	0.049	0.044	0.039	0.032	0.025	0.015	0.009	0.006	0.003
15	0.861	0.743	0.555	0.417	0.315	0.239	0.183	0.140	0.123	0.108	0.084	0.065	0.051	0.040	0.035	0.031	0.025	0.020	0.011	0.006	0.004	0.002
16	0.853	0.728	0.534	0.394	0.292	0.218	0.163	0.123	0.107	0.093	0.071	0.054	0.042	0.032	0.028	0.025	0.019	0.015	0.008	0.005	0.003	0.002
17	0.844	0.714	0.513	0.371	0.270	0.198	0.146	0.108	0.093	0.080	0.060	0.045	0.034	0.026	0.023	0.020	0.015	0.012	0.006	0.003	0.002	0.001
18	0.836	0.700	0.494	0.350	0.250	0.180	0.130	0.095	0.081	0.069	0.051	0.038	0.028	0.021	0.018	0.016	0.012	0.009	0.005	0.002	0.001	0.001
19	0.828	0.686	0.475	0.331	0.232	0.164	0.116	0.083	0.070	0.060	0.043	0.031	0.023	0.017	0.014	0.012	0.009	0.007	0.003	0.002	0.001	
20	0.820	0.673	0.456	0.312	0.215	0.149	0.104	0.073	0.061	0.051	0.037	0.026	0.019	0.014	0.012	0.010	0.007	0.005	0.002	0.001	0.001	
21	0.811	0.660	0.439	0.294	0.199	0.135	0.093	0.064	0.053	0.044	0.031	0.022	0.015	0.011	0.009	0.008	0.006	0.004	0.002	0.001		
22	0.803	0.647	0.422	0.278	0.184	0.123	0.083	0.056	0.046	0.038	0.026	0.018	0.013	0.009	0.007	0.006	0.004	0.003	0.001	0.001		
23	0.795	0.634	0.406	0.262	0.170	0.112	0.074	0.049	0.040	0.033	0.022	0.015	0.010	0.007	0.006	0.005	0.003	0.002	0.001			
24	0.788	0.622	0.390	0.247	0.158	0.102	0.066	0.043	0.035	0.028	0.019	0.013	0.008	0.006	0.005	0.004	0.003	0.002	0.001			
25	0.780	0.610	0.375	0.233	0.146	0.092	0.059	0.038	0.030	0.024	0.016	0.010	0.007	0.005	0.004	0.003	0.002	0.001	0.001			
26	0.772	0.598	0.361	0.220	0.135	0.084	0.053	0.033	0.026	0.021	0.014	0.009	0.006	0.004	0.003	0.002	0.002	0.001				
27	0.764	0.586	0.347	0.207	0.125	0.076	0.047	0.029	0.023	0.018	0.011	0.007	0.005	0.003	0.002	0.002	0.001	0.001				
28	0.757	0.574	0.333	0.196	0.116	0.069	0.042	0.026	0.020	0.016	0.010	0.006	0.004	0.002	0.002	0.002	0.001	0.001				
29	0.749	0.563	0.321	0.185	0.107	0.063	0.037	0.022	0.017	0.014	0.008	0.005	0.003	0.002	0.002	0.001	0.001	0.001				
30	0.742	0.552	0.308	0.174	0.099	0.057	0.033	0.020	0.015	0.012	0.007	0.004	0.003	0.002	0.001	0.001	0.001	0.001				

seven. Continuing the example, asset B could be an automated pizza baker costing $12,000 that would be the most
productive (have the greatest ROI) toward the latter part of
its ten-year life because its total output capacity wouldn't be
fully utilized until that time. Again, we'll assume no salvage
value at the end of year 10. Realistically, your company might
profitably use either of these capital assets, but you can't afford to acquire both of them at once. Which should you buy?
Or should you pass up the opportunity for either?

We'll assume the same ROI yearly for these assets that we
used when calculating their payback (see Table 4). Also, we'll
use the present value factors shown in the 4 percent and 6
percent columns of Table 6. As can be seen, these calculations

Table 6. Comparative ROI analysis of a dough

Asset A (dough mixer)

	Yearly Contribution	*4% Factor*	*Trial Present Value of Contribution*	*6% Factor*	*Trial Present Value of Contribution*
1st year	$ 2,500	.962	$ 2,405	.943	$ 2,358
2nd year	2,500	.925	2,313	.890	2,225
3rd year	2,000	.889	1,778	.840	1,680
4th year	1,750	.855	1,496	.792	1,386
5th year	1,250	.822	1,028	.747	934
6th year	1,000	.790	790	.705	705
7th year	1,000	.760	760	.665	665
Totals	$12,000		$10,570		$ 9,953

Initial Cost of Dough Mixer	10,000	10,000
Net Present Value of Contribution	$570	($47)

Calculation of Projected Rate of Return:
    $570 + $47 = $617
    570 ÷ 617 = .924
    .924 × 2% (span between 4% and 6%) = 1.848, or 1.85%
    4% + 1.85% = 5.85% = ROI

produce an interesting but somewhat unexpected result. The dough mixer will produce a slightly higher ROI than the automated baker, even though the latter will generate $3,500 more contribution. Would you have anticipated the outcome? The reason, of course, has to do with the higher initial cost for the automated baker and the longer time it requires to produce its total contribution.

In short, then, the dough mixer is a better investment because it has the greater profitability. But is its return enough to justify purchase? Considering that the cost of money (the interest charged for most commercial loans) has been holding steady at above 7 percent, an investment of $10,000 that will produce a return of only 5.85% would be

mixer (asset A) and automated baker (asset B).

			Asset B (automated baker)		
	Yearly Contribution	*4% Factor*	*Trial Present Value of Contribution*	*6% Factor*	*Trial Present Value of Contribution*
1st year	$ 1,000	.962	$ 962	.943	$ 943
2nd year	1,500	.925	1,388	.890	1,335
3rd year	1,500	.889	1,334	.840	1,260
4th year	2,000	.855	1,710	.792	1,584
5th year	2,000	.822	1,644	.747	1,494
6th year	2,500	.790	1,975	.705	1,763
7th year	2,000	.760	1,520	.665	1,330
8th year	1,000	.731	731	.627	627
9th year	1,000	.703	703	.592	592
10th year	1,000	.676	676	.558	558
Totals	$15,500		$12,643		$11,486

Initial Cost of Automated Baker   12,000   12,000
Net Present Value of Contribution $643   ($514)

Calculation of Projected Rate of Return:
     $643 + $514 = $1,157
     $643 ÷ $1,157 = .556
     .556 × 2% (span between 4% and 6%) = 1.112 or 1.11%
     4% + 1.11% = 5.11% = ROI

very questionable. The only reason for making such a purchase would be if the dough mixer were considered absolutely
indispensable to the entire pizzeria supply operation. Even
then, other elements of the production process would have to
generate enough profitability to make up for its poor showing.

This concludes the explanation of the discounted cash-
flow evaluation. If you have followed it carefully, you should
have formed an opinion regarding this approach. You may
not like it, feeling that it's too complicated. But a more useful
way to appraise it is to ask yourself how much effort is worthwhile, considering that a possible expenditure of $10,000 to
$12,000 is under consideration. Now that both techniques
have been explained, it can be seen that the discounted cash-
flow technique is a far more useful approach to investment
analysis than the payback method.

Establishing an Asset's ROI Contribution

So far in this chapter, we have discussed the dollar
amounts of asset ROI contributions as though they were easily derived. Back in the introduction of this chapter, we even
introduced a formula for calculating the ROI for an asset,
namely

$$\text{Asset ROI} = \frac{\text{average contribution to profit}}{\text{amount of investment}}$$

What an innocent-sounding definition, considering how hard
it can be to come up with a realistic estimate for the future
profit contribution of an asset! In point of fact, this is the most
difficult part of the whole process.

There are several reasons for this. First of all, we are dealing with the future, and who knows exactly what it will hold?
What will the health of the U.S. economy be like in five or ten
years? How will your state and/or city be affected? What about
your competition—will it be the same, better, or worse? (If

business gets bad, the profit contribution actually produced by an asset may drop far below what was expected.)

Second, asset ROI estimates are often based on manufacturers' claims concerning the rated output of a machine, for example, or the comparative efficiency of two kinds of processes. Even if we eliminate the possibility of exaggerated claims or even outright deception, we still cannot ignore the fact that a manufacturer's estimate is generally based on ideal operating conditions. This includes a constant flow of work, high-quality material, well-trained operators, and an efficient work environment. Does your company have all of these things all of the time? Probably not, so you should include a "fudge factor" before you use a manufacturer's claim in determining asset ROI.

Finally, there are other possible negative influences, such as a changing public demand for your product or service, repressive acts of government, poor labor relations, natural catastrophes, and, last but not least, managerial mistakes that you may make in the future.

For all of these reasons, you will find that the future asset ROI estimating process can only be a guess. Do the best you can—make it an intelligent guess, including as many *known* factors as possible—but also recognize that you are guessing when you estimate annual savings for the capital asset under consideration.

Conclusion

When we compared the desirability of various kinds of costs, we computed the present value of money expected to be received or spent in the future at different rates of discount. As noted during the discussion, those discount rates must be taken into consideration by you, the owner or manager. On the other hand, there is always an element of risk involved— any decision regarding the future is risky. When you compare different proposals for capital expenditures, you cannot ignore the differences in risk that the various assets represent.

As a general rule, risk becomes greater as the number of years extends further into the future. For this reason a fairly rapid payback of the capital investment is often very attractive. However, as we have seen, to insist on quick payback *may* result in a less profitable capital asset. To make more profit you often have to risk a greater chance of failure. All decisions regarding capital expenditures include some risk, but by using the techniques discussed in this chapter, the degree of risk can be cut down.

SECTION IV

Building an Estate
from Your Business

9

How Valuable
Is Your Business?

FROM a strictly financial point of view, your business is simply an *investment opportunity*, which could be either more or less valuable to you than some alternative use of the same money. The information contained in this chapter will enable you to determine just how valuable your "stake" or equity in the company would be to an impartial observer. You might then want to think about other uses for the money.

Of course, such a "cold cash" concept disregards any personal sentiments you may have about the future of the business. But that might not be bad. At times, personal feelings can override sound business judgment. So keep in mind, if you will, the theme of this chapter—that an unbiased financial valuation ought to be developed and done periodically for *any* ongoing business concern, including yours.

You will learn in the next few pages how a business's value is computed. You might even attempt to try it yourself. In any case, you will be better able to understand what is happening if you pay someone else to work out the valuation.

In addition to an owner's examination of his or her firm's current value, there are five other occasions when a business valuation is commonly carried out:

1. When a company is to be bought or sold.
2. When a company goes bankrupt.
3. When a company is trying to attract new equity capital.
4. When the company's owner takes out "key man insurance" to protect his or her personal equity in the business for the benefit of specified heirs.
5. When either #1 or #4 is being considered, but no final decision has yet been reached.

Before we begin to discuss the different valuation methods, let's briefly consider another aspect of small-business management which relates to the value of a business. Many small companies are deliberately operated to make less than the maximum possible profit. The owner may in some cases take on tax-deductible expenses in order to hold down the taxable income of the company. In effect, the business is managed so as to serve as a *tax shelter* for the owner. For instance, an owner might spend considerable money taking business guests on a trip and then write off the cost against "customer entertainment" or "sales promotion" or something similar. The same thing is involved when an owner has the business buy something for his own personal, nonbusiness use. Examples range all the way from a station wagon that the owner might use during off-hours, to a camera that could be taken on a vacation.

Any or all of such business costs are "artificial" from the standpoint of profitability. Therefore, when a valuation computation is being performed for a business with artificially reduced profits, a restatement of earnings is appropriate. You will know if such a restatement is warranted when your own business is being valued; with another business, you can make an intelligent guess if you carefully examine all the accounting records. In either case, the necessary recalculation of earnings is relatively simple since it involves merely the elimination of various nonbusiness expenses from the official income statement, thus producing an increase in the amount of pretax profit that would have been earned had such costs not been incurred.

The Importance of a Satisfactory Return on Investment

The rate at which any company *should* be earning involves (at least in part) a subjective judgment. We dealt with return on investment (ROI) to a considerable extent in Chapter 8, but didn't confront the question of a *proper* rate of return. That's because there is no such thing, strictly speaking. If you are satisfied with the ROI of your business, that's all that matters. However, two questions are appropriate at this point: (1) Do you really know your present rate of income compared to your total business equity? (2) If you are interested in buying a company, is there a "target" earnings rate that you expect the newly acquired business to reach? To answer either of these questions accurately requires that a business valuation be undertaken. Such a valuation would focus on the *real worth* of the company (assets minus liabilities) and on its *earnings potential*.

First, let's examine the valuation procedures that can produce answers to the above questions. This will be done using the "objective" (that is, factual) approach. Then we'll conclude with a discussion of the way that either a buyer or a seller is likely to look at the typical business valuation.

How Company Assets Are Valued

There are three common methods of determining the worth of the assets of a closely held business. These are their *book value*, their *liquidation value*, and their *market value* (or *adjusted book value*).

In most cases, the *book value* of assets can be derived directly from a company's accounting records. It is whatever the net value of the assets is shown to be on the balance sheet. Generally speaking, book value is not acceptable for valuation purposes except in the case of cash. The reason is that in view of various technological developments and also because of the constant influence of inflation, the book value may be too high if an asset has become technologically obsolete or too low if the market price of the asset is on the rise.

Just as book value is not a good measure of business asset worth, so *liquidation value* is not a realistic way to determine how much equity remains in any company's assets. This is best illustrated by an analogy. You no doubt have a favorite couch at home that you like because of its initial cost, comfort, style, consistency with the rest of the decor, and so on. Furthermore, let's say it's only a year or two old, hardly used. Even so, how much do you suppose a second-hand furniture dealer would pay for it? Not anything near its value to you and certainly nothing approaching the current cost of a new couch. For a buyer of second-hand furniture, there is always the possibility of prior misuse, and at best there is an ill-defined resale market for it. The same applies to used business assets. Even if you could determine the theoretical liquidation value of your business assets without offering them for sale, you couldn't in reality use those figures to indicate the worth of the business, because the test of marketability has not been applied.

The only realistic way to establish values for the assets of a business concern is to start with their book value and then add or subtract an adjusting factor. The result is called *adjusted book value* or real market value. Below are some commonly accepted ways for you or your bookkeeper to adjust the book values of particular asset categories:

Accounts receivable. Subtract an allowance for the failure of some of your credit customers to pay their bills. About 5 percent of current receivables is considered realistic.

Raw materials inventory. Add or subtract in accordance with the difference between what you paid for items now in stock and their current market price. Remember, this difference will vary with fluctuations in the market, but don't worry about it. You are establishing a one-time value for the purpose of assessing your business equity as of the moment, and also as the basis for establishing your current ROI.

Work-in-process inventory. Start with your most recent balance-sheet amount. If you granted a general pay increase to your employees, increase the work-in-process value by the same percent as that used in calculating the pay increase. Otherwise, increase by one percent to allow for random merit raises.

Finished goods inventory. Your accounting records will very likely show these items at cost. Refigure at selling price for use in the asset valuation process.

Supplies. The comments made for raw material inventory also apply to supplies.

Capital assets and facilities. Start with their depreciated book value. Add a factor to indicate their appreciation due to inflation, except in those cases where you know that a particular item has been made obsolete by some recent technological improvement. In such instances, don't change the depreciated book value.

If you don't want to guess at an asset appreciation percentage, find out from your local board of realtors the rate of appreciation they use in establishing the resale price of private homes. Use that rate for *all* of your capital assets and facilities (accountants often employ the term *fixed assets* for such items) and you won't be very far off. Once you've computed the adjusted value for all of your assets, you must subtract the amount of current and long-term liabilities. The end result will be your adjusted equity in the business.

How Prospects for Business Profitability Are Evaluated

There are two ways to assess the profit potential of your business: you can base it either on what you *know* has happened in the past or on what you *expect* to happen in the years ahead. It follows that there are two different methods of valuing a business based on its estimated earning power. The methods are termed *capitalization of past earnings* and *discounting of future earnings*. Both rely on the asset valuation which we discussed as part of the profitability equation. The other ingredient of that equation is an approximation of either the past or the future stream of profits.

The more conservative profitability calculation is that which looks to the past. Depending upon individual circumstances, either the most recent year's profit or an average of the last four or five years' profits may be used. The latter is preferable unless there has been an unusual earnings pattern making it unrealistic to include the earlier years. The logic behind this computation is simply that recent business profits should count as much as the owner's present equity in the assets when a company's true value is being determined.

The profit-valuation procedure is best described as a two-step process: first, calculate the actual rate of profitability and compare it to what a potential investor would like it to be; then develop an "adjusted" rate and use the latter in the "capitalizing" calculation. Let's take a closer look at these two steps.

1. Your actual profitability rate can be obtained by using the formula:

$$\text{ROI} = \frac{\text{annual profit (or 4 or 5 years' average profit)}}{\text{owner's equity}}$$

The calculation will be most realistic if actual profit rather than any restatement of the profit is used in the numerator of the fraction. It will also be more realistic if the total owner's equity as shown on the latest balance sheet (rather than the net adjusted asset valuation described earlier in this chapter) is entered as the denominator. You will find that the answer developed by this computation will be similar to that derived in calculating the return on net worth discussed in Chapter 6.

Now, depending upon the stability of your company and the appeal of your product or service, an outside investor would probably require that your ROI be somewhere in the range of 20 to 50 percent. Was your actual ROI that high? Most small companies would be very satisfied to be in the 10–15 percent range. Some operate at even lower levels. So if your calculated ROI is anywhere from 10 to 50 percent, you are in the ball park. However, if your ROI is on the low side, you might adjust the rate upward by 10 percent or so to be more consistent with outside expectations.

2. Your next move is to apply the adjusted ROI rate to average profit or to last year's profit. Compare the result with the adjusted asset valuation, which was explained in the previous section of this chapter. This will provide an illustration of the benefit of capitalization of fast earnings. You may or may not find that this method produces a higher valuation than that derived by simply adjusting the book value of your assets. Bear both methods in mind later in the chapter when we discuss setting a selling price on your business.

If the trend in your earnings has been gradually upward over the past few years, you can usually derive an even more satisfactory valuation (that is, better than the capitalization of past earnings) by discounting estimated future earnings in accordance with their present value. This is also something to be considered when establishing a selling price for a business.

An Example of Valuation Calculations

In order to help you comprehend the arithmetic involved in each of the business valuation procedures just described, a simplified example is shown in Figures 14–16. The figures highlight the essential income and equity data and adjusted balance-sheet values. You should have no difficulty seeing that important differences exist between the balance sheet totals as of December 31, 1977, and the adjusted totals calculated for valuation purposes as of April 30, 1978. The net amount of the increase in value is $21,017. The reasons for this improvement are:

- The pace of business picked up from January to April, creating shifts up and down in many of the accounts.

- Accounts receivable was reduced to allow for a nominal number of bad debts.
- The market price of the inventory increased by 10 percent during the period.
- There was about an 8 percent appreciation in market value of the property and equipment, which offset normal depreciation and resulted in an upward revision in the book value of these assets.

All the changes illustrated so far are based on *past* values. A capitalization of recent earnings plus a projection of the earning potential for the future are often considered to be even more useful, since these may provide a higher current value of the business. The respective calculations are shown in Figures 17–19.

The 32 percent rate of return derived in Figure 17 is very satisfactory. In Figure 18 the rate has been raised to 35 percent to show the capitalization calculation. This produces a small increase in recognition of the steady growth of earnings over the past several years.

You will notice that in neither case have we reached a figure equal to the adjusted total net worth of $133,412 that was derived in Figure 16. Thus, in this case, the adjustments of book values from the balance sheet produce a higher cur-

Figure 14. B. L. Smith Electrical Contractors—Comparative schedule of sales, after-tax income, and net worth.

Year	Sales	Net Income	Total Net Worth
1973	312,865	35,500	95,330
1974	304,240	28,110	97,990
1975	309,180	32,850	101,755
1976	317,405	39,700	105,405
1977	323,790	42,250	112,395

Figure 15. B. L. Smith Electrical Contractors—Balance sheet, December 31, 1977.

ASSETS

Current Assets		
Cash	$27,500	
Notes and accounts receivable	4,350	
Costs in excess of billings	15,300	
Unused inventories	57,250	
Prepaid expenses	890	
Total current assets		$105,290
Capital Assets		
Property and equipment—net	75,380	75,380
Other Assets		
Workmen's comp. insur. deposit	2,225	
Claim for refund—fed. inc. tax	5,000	
Total other assets		7,225
Total Assets		$187,895

LIABILITIES

Current Liabilities		
Accounts payable	31,820	
Billings in excess of cost	2,750	
Current portion, long-term debt	5,500	
Accruals		
Payroll taxes and withholdings	660	
State and local taxes	770	
Total current liabilities		$ 41,500
Fixed Liabilities		
Long-term debt—bank	34,000	34,000
Net worth		
Stockholders' equity—common stock	69,500	
" " —preferred stock	8,500	
Retained earnings	34,395	
Total Net Worth		112,395
Total Liabilities and Net Worth		$187,895

Figure 16a. B. L. Smith Electrical Contractors—Balance sheet adjustments for assets, December 31, 1977.

ASSETS	From 1977 Balance Sheet	Adjustment	Adjusted Balance Sheet
Current Assets			
Cash	$ 27,500		$ 18,850
4-30-78 trial bal.— reduction		(8,650)	
Notes and accounts receivable	4,350		4,132
4-30-78 trial bal.— decrease 5%		(218)	
Costs in excess of billings	15,300		6,050
4-30-78 trial bal.— reduction		(9,250)	
Unused inventories	57,250		83,800
4-30-78 trial bal.— increase		18,950	
Increased market price—10%		7,600	
Prepaid expenses	890		1,560
4-30-78 trial bal.— increase		530	
Increased market price—10%		140	
Total Current Assets	105,290		114,392
Capital Assets			
Property and equipment—net	75,380		82,290
4-15-78 physical apprai- sal—increase		6,910	
Other Assets			
Workmen's comp. insur. de- posit	2,225		1,000
4-30-78 trial bal.— reduction		(1,225)	
Claim for refund—fed. inc. tax	5,000		0
4-30-78 trial bal.— reduction		(5,000)	
Total Assets	$187,895		$197,682
Net valuation adjust- ments to assets		$ 9,787	

Figure 16*b*. B. L. Smith Electrical Contractors—Balance sheet adjustments for liabilities, December 31, 1977.

LIABILITIES	From 1977 Balance Sheet	Adjust- ment	Adjusted Balance Sheet
Balance forward		$ 9,787	
Current Liabilities			
Accounts payable	$ 31,820		$ 28,670
4-30-78 trial bal.— reduction		3,150	
Billings in excess of cost	2,750		0
4-30-78 trial bal.— reduction		2,750	
Current portion, long-term debt	5,500		
4-30-78 trial bal.— reduction		5,500	0
Accruals			
Payroll taxes and with-holding	660		680
4-30-78 trial bal.— increase		(20)	
State and local taxes	770		920
4-30-78 trial bal.— increase		(150)	
Total Current Liabilities	$ 41,500		$ 30,270
Fixed Liabilities			
Long-term debt—bank	34,000		34,000
Net Worth			
Stockholders' equity— common stock	69,500		69,500
Stockholders' equity— preferred stock	8,500		8,500
Retained earnings	34,395		34,395
Valuation surplus—net		$21,017	
Total Net Worth	112,395		133,412
Total Liabilities and Net Worth	$187,895		$197,682

Figure 17. Calculation of past profitability rate.

Average income, 1973 through 1977 (from Figure 14):

1973	$ 35,500
1974	28,110
1975	32,850
1976	39,700
1977	42,250

$178,410 ÷ 5 = $35,682 Average earnings for last 5 years

$112,395 = Actual owners' equity, 1977 (from Figure 15)

$$\text{ROI} = \frac{\$35,682}{\$112,395} = .317 \times 100 = 31.7 \text{ or } 32\%$$

rent valuation. However, by discounting future earnings (in Figure 19), we obtain the highest valuation of all. A future-earnings discount of 15 percent is considerably more than the current cost to borrow but it may well be that high by 1982, the final year of our future projection.

If you were contemplating the sale of a business such as the B. L. Smith Electrical Contractors Co. (described in Figures 14–19), the valuation developed in Figure 19 could logically be selected as your asking price. The same value should also be utilized if a "key man" insurance policy were to be written on the life o B. L. Smith, with insurance premiums paid by the firm.

On the other hand, if you were considering buying the B. L. Smith company, you might make an offer in accordance with the value shown in Figures 16 or 17. Either of these would also be realistic if an analysis was made of this company for general information purposes (or possibly to compare the present worth with a value established at some earlier date).

In other words, the *purpose* of valuation, as well as the *method*, will always be significant. The choice is up to you. Any

Figure 18. Capitalization of past earnings at 35 percent.

A. On average income, 1973 through 1977:
Average income = \$35,682 (from Figure 17)
$$\frac{\$35,682}{.35} = \$101,949$$

B. On 1977 income:
$$\frac{\$42,250}{.35} = \$120,714$$

of the procedures illustrated in this chapter will produce a realistic result. Now, you might try working out a valuation for your own business; the information gained will be very useful.

Figure 19. Discounting of future earnings at 15 percent.

$$\text{Increase per year} = \frac{1977 \text{ income} - 1973 \text{ income}}{\text{number of years}}$$
$$= \frac{\$42,250 - \$35,500}{5} = \frac{\$6,750}{5} = \$1,350$$

Past income growth based on 1977 income
$$= \frac{\$1,350}{\$42,250} = 3\% \text{ per year}$$

Assume future income growth of 3% per year for next five years:

	15% Discount Factor	Present Value of Future Income
Estimated income 1978 = \$43,518 ×	0.870 =	\$37,861
1979 = \$44,824 ×	0.756 =	\$33,887
1980 = \$46,169 ×	0.658 =	\$30,379
1981 = \$47,554 ×	0.572 =	\$27,201
1982 = \$48,981 ×	0.497 =	\$24,344
Total present value of est. future income		\$153,672

Conclusion

As we have seen, business valuations can mean different things to different people, and their significance can vary depending on why the valuation was computed. Too conservative a valuation (too low) can cause financial hardship if you want to attract a buyer for the firm or are seeking expansion of equity through a sale of partial ownership. Too liberal a valuation (too high) could possibly be considered fraudulent. Both of these are to be avoided.

Perhaps the best way to regard any valuation of your business is: *"What is my business's value to me?"* The introduction to this chapter indicated that business is simply an investment opportunity. Clearly, your business isn't worth less than what you can sell it for. Equally clearly, the business should not be valued higher than what it would cost you to replace it. If you can approximate the lower and upper value boundaries, you will have the most realistic understanding of the worth of the business you now own or any other business you may want to buy. This chapter has attempted to explain the process of finding those lower and upper limits.

From the long-range point of view (if you can step back from daily operations far enough to adopt such a view), your primary problem as a business manager is not only to increase your company's income but also to increase the company's *value*. If you look at it in that way, then current income is only one of several ways to measure growth in value. Another way is to determine *future potential* for earnings. Here, you could deliberately minimize current profit by spending money now on more efficient facilities that will increase profitability in the future and that will also last a long time. However, when you make a decision like that, it helps to know approximately what the business is worth *right now*. Such information is fairly easily developed from the valuation methods discussed in this chapter.

10

Preplanning
the Disposition
of Your Business

JUST as you know that the sun will rise tomorrow, you should also realize that some day you'll be out of business—either because you want to be or because you are forced to be. Since it's certain, why not be foresighted and get ready to dispose of your business *now*? When the time finally comes, the disposition process will take considerable advance preparation or negotiation, assuming you will want to work out the best possible deal. However, if you have carried out your preliminary disposition plan each step of the way—with occasional modifications to accommodate economic or other changes—you will be able to sell or give up your company without sacrifice. Let that be your goal.

Rest assured—if you don't plan, if you don't prepare

ahead of time, you're going to be sorry. Or it will be your heirs who will be hurt. Every day, somewhere in this country a number of small-business owners (or their heirs) discover what can happen to a "going" business if death or disability occurs unexpectedly and there was no advance preparation for an orderly transfer of ownership. At such times, assets usually must be disposed of quickly and at considerable loss; future security is often given up or greatly diminished; sometimes, the rightful heirs are denied access to the property for months or even years. In extreme cases, the company goes out of business, and the former owner's family must fall back on cash savings or borrow to make ends meet. Living standards are reduced, comfort vanishes, and so on. Not a pleasant prospect, is it? How much better to get ready well in advance, when the business is still reasonably profitable and while you are still fully in control.

Possible Methods of Disposition

Very few owners or operators want to simply close up shop. Most want their business to go on functioning even after they no longer have an interest in it. That's the approach which we will take in this discussion. We'll assume that you would like the business to be eventually handed over either to your family or transferred to unrelated new owners. The principal question is, What options are available and what's involved with each?

Following are some of the ways in which the ownership of a business may be given up by the original owner (or group of owners):

1. *Taken over upon the death or disability of one of the owners by the remaining partners or shareholders.* This approach is very frequently arranged through the use of "key man" insurance, which makes the company the beneficiary. Then, at the time of death or disability, the company receives the proceeds of the policy and thus can pay off the estate of the dead or disabled individual without seriously depleting working capi-

tal. Obviously, advance collaboration with an insurance broker is essential here.

2. *Taken over by relatives or friends.* This approach presents a number of different possibilities. The relatives or friends may buy the business outright, in which case the original owner may be subject to capital gains tax. Alternatively, the original owner may give away his ownership, which may make the recipients subject to a gift tax. Or the original owner may transfer ownership to a trust, along with a directive that the trust oversee operation of the business and control distribution of the profits to relatives or friends. This last option is generally used when there are a number of heirs and the original owner has some strong preference as to the final division of the business assets. (In that case, inheritance tax may be involved, or at least income tax may be payable on the profits.) With any of these choices there is a definite need to plan in advance with the help of an attorney.

3. *Taken over by a group of top-level employees.* This approach could involve a buy-out, but it is much more frequently arranged through a trust, such as an employee stock ownership trust (ESOT). An ESOT permits the original owner to get his investment back, to realize the benefit of appreciated business value (and pay only capital gains tax), and at the same time to keep control of the business. This is a very complex transaction involving collaboration with an attorney and a bank or other financial institution. It is discussed more fully in the next section of this chapter.

With the help of your attorney, your banker, and/or your insurance broker, it will be possible to prearrange the disposition of your business to best suit your future interests. The above examples are merely intended to illustrate the range of your available choices.

Protecting the Interests of Your Key Employees

Considered in one way, your company is simply a group of people. However, any business that is functioning and profitable always consists of more than just a group. At the very least, your key employees are likely to have special training, experience, and motivation. In short, they may be more accurately described as a *team*. Nevertheless, they are individuals with their own complex and shifting personal problems and values.

In thinking about disposing of your business, it is suggested that you bear two factors in mind. First, the management team may not share your point of view regarding the benefits of transferring ownership. (In fact, they almost certainly will not. They know where they stand with you, but what will their status be with the next owner?) Second, you undoubtedly place great reliance on these key people. Suppose their performance declines? Worse still, suppose one or more should quit and start a business for himself which is similar to yours, or even go to work for one of your competitors? It is quite possible for a so-called "well-oiled" business team to more or less disintegrate or at least to suffer a considerable loss of efficiency *if the key team members feel uncertain about their own futures.*

For this reason, you should give careful consideration to selecting a plan for disposing of the business which safeguards the future of the key team members as much as possible. You may decide that any particular approach is too complex, too costly, or simply not for you. On the other hand, you should at least know a little about the possible alternatives.

Currently, a very popular way to enhance a feeling of security on the part of your management team is to set up an employee stock ownership trust (ESOT) in their behalf. This approach has become possible as the result of recent tax legislation. With this arrangement, you gradually transfer your ownership into the custody of the ESOT by selling shares of your stock to it over a period of time. The ESOT obtains the money to pay for your stock by borrowing, by receiving contributions from the employees who are to benefit from it, or by receiving payments from the company itself. Incidentally, the last mentioned payments are tax deductible for the company, and since there is then no overall cost to the company, it has become by far the most popular way to set up an ESOT.

An ESOT can offer important advantages to both the present owner(s) and the participating employees. Let us consider a few of these.

Benefits of an ESOT to the Owner(s)

• No loss of managerial control, since the trust can be established to require its administrative committee to vote the acquired stock in accordance with the original owner's wishes. Alternatively, the shares transferred to the ESOT can be a special "nonvoting" type of common stock.

• Provides for ESOT compensation to the original owner at a fair market value for the stock, that is, at a price established by an independent valuation process.

• Permits the original owner to pay only capital gains tax, rather than straight income tax, for payments received against the appreciated value of the transferred stock.

• Gradually builds employees' ownership of the company, thus stimulating a managerial attitude and a feeling of unity on their part. Serves as an effective incentive for employees to upgrade their performance.

Benefits of an ESOT to Participating Employees

• No reduction in employee's take-home pay (unless the employee-contribution option is chosen as the method of purchasing the stock).

• Growth of an employee's interest in the company is not subject to taxation until actual distribution of his ownership share in the company to him or his heirs. This distribution normally takes place at death or retirement.

Benefits to the Company

There are a number of financial advantages that the company itself might gain through use of the ESOT approach.

(Some of these will require prior approval of the Internal Revenue Service; check before proceeding.)

• Suppose the company needs to obtain additional equity capital. Since the ESOT already owns company stock, the trust borrows the needed amount of money from a bank, buys more authorized (but previously unissued) stock from the company, and then pledges the stock as collateral for the loan. The company can guarantee the ESOT loan if this is desired by the bank. Since the ESOT already has a source of financial contributions, either from the company or the employees, some of this income may be used to discharge the bank loan.

• Suppose that the company wants to acquire ownership of another company. Again, the ESOT can borrow enough from a bank to buy the other company's stock. It then exchanges the stock just purchased for additional authorized (but previously unissued) stock of the original company. Furnishing security and repaying the bank loan would be the same as explained above.

• Suppose the company intends to take out substantial life insurance policies on key employees and to pay the premiums. Current IRS policy is that these premium payments may not be taken as a tax-deductible expense by the company. However, with an ESOT, life insurance costs can be drastically reduced. It works like this: the company makes the regular, nondeductible insurance premium payments, and in the same year donates an equivalent dollar value of authorized but previously unissued stock to ESOT; this stock donation is deductible from the company's income tax and has the effect of offsetting the expense of the insurance premium.

• Suppose the company has funds held in a profit-sharing fund and wants to withdraw the money for one or more capital improvements without harming the interests of the key employees who expect to benefit when the proceeds are later distributed. This can be accomplished by converting the profit-sharing plan to an ESOT. The profit-sharing funds can then be used for the purchase of authorized but previously unissued stock of the company. The company gets access to the money free and clear; the ESOT now holds the company's stock for the benefit of the employees.

With all of the possibilities described above (and a few somewhat more complex measures which have not been described), it is certainly worth your while to investigate the ESOT approach when planning to set up your estate. A properly established ESOT can benefit you, your key employees, and your company.

Transferring Your Ownership into the Custody of a Trust

This approach is commonly adopted when a business owner does not want the company management to be taken over by his heirs, even though he wishes to keep the ownership within the family. An ESOT, as discussed above, would not be set up, since such a device shifts ownership to the employees.

This may be the owner's way of protecting the estate from incurring losses due to mismanagement; it may even be the only way, in the owner's judgment, to keep the business from being dissolved. In any case, the title to the business passes to a trustee (or trust company) who then administers the company according to the terms of the trust, for the benefit of the family or other designated individuals. This means that the trustee must:

- Protect the business by ensuring that it is managed properly.
- Try to carry out the intention of the trust agreement with respect to the distribution of income.
- Attempt to retain all of the business's value for the benefit of the eventual heirs, who will inherit the assets when the trust is finally terminated.

Quite a tall order to expect a trustee to accomplish these things, don't you agree? Usually only a well-established trust company (such as a bank) can provide the capable management needed.

From your standpoint, great care should be taken to select a trustee who can be expected to fulfill the role successfully. If you choose a bank, you should be aware that bank employees are often, by nature and by training, very conservative. Thus, it may be that the results (in terms of income or long-term growth) will be less than your heirs expect. Also, you should understand that once an institution is named as trustee, the beneficiaries cannot "unname" that trustee regardless of the reason.

Another dual benefit that you can provide your heirs by designating a trustee rather than simply willing the business directly to them is the *avoidance of probate* and a *savings in inheritance taxes*. Unfortunately, the tax savings will not amount to much unless your estate exceeds $200,000. (If you own your home in addition to the business, your net estate total could easily be valued at that figure or even higher.) The most popular way to proceed is to divide the business owner-ship between husband and wife. This is something you might want to consider early in the life of the company because to wait until a few years before retirement is to risk an IRS ruling that the ownership change was made solely for the purpose of tax evasion. Once the division is legally ac-complished, the ownership share belonging to each spouse can then be left in trust to children or other heirs. After the death of one of the spouses, the survivor can, if desired, with-draw a percentage of the other's estate in trust in order to maintain his or her customary standard of living. Thus, there is no financial detriment of any sort to this approach.

Another form of trust agreement you might consider is the so-called "living" trust which, as the name implies, goes into effect while you are still alive. With this type of trust, you can retire, turn the business over to the trustee, and begin to receive income from the trust during your retirement. The income then goes to your heirs, in any manner you designate, upon your death. In the meantime, since you would be the grantor of the trust, you could revoke it, reduce it, enlarge it, or change it any way you see fit. Thus, this type of trust can provide the basis for a coordinated and flexible retirement plan for you, as well as a way to arrange for the management and distribution of your business assets upon your death.

Conclusion

This chapter has stressed the need to preplan the way your business will finally be disposed of. Looking ahead also involves decisions as to (a) who your heirs will be and (b) how much of your total estate you want each heir to receive. The three advisors who can help you most with these decisions are your banker (or investment counselor), lawyer, and insurance broker. However, even after the disposition plans have been worked out, don't make the mistake of believing that the job is finished once and for all. You should review (and possibly reconsider) earlier decisions each time there is a marriage, birth, or death involving members of your family. Also, when the size of your company or its level of profitability is significantly changed, another look at the disposition scheme is warranted.

Essentially, you need to be aware that over the long run your business success really creates *two* estates. The one which is most readily apparent is your "living" estate, composed of your present business ownership and any other assets. The other estate could be termed "death" estate—the money and assets that your heirs will receive when you die or become totally disabled. Many small businessmen pay a disproportionate share of attention to their "living" estate, watching it grow and prosper and then enjoying the fruits of their efforts. But that can be a mistake. Don't concentrate so exclusively on making the business go that you forget what could happen to your family's security when you die. You can never know how much benefit—or how much grief—will result in the future from what you do or don't do while still actively running the business.

SECTION V

Administering Your Firm's Profitability

11

Surviving Bankruptcy

IF you are a member of the old school, you've probably re-
garded bankruptcy with all the dread of a serious illness—you
know it can happen, but you'd just as soon not think about it!
Perhaps you knew someone years ago whose company went
through the process, and you still remember what a disgrace
it was to go bankrupt.

Well, in case you haven't noticed, times have changed.
Bankruptcy is no longer synonymous with failure. In fact, if
you knew the complete financial background of the most successful business concerns in your area, you'd find that a sur-
prisingly high percentage of them had been bankrupt sometime during their early years, and in a few cases, more than
once.

Actually, bankruptcy can be a means of business survival,
rather than business extinction, when entered into at an appropriate time. Just as a business owner might decide to borrow from a bank to solve a financial crisis, he or she might
instead elect to petition for voluntary bankruptcy. This could

occur, for example, as the aftermath of a natural disaster. It might also take place as the result of failure on the part of several major customers, after losing a large lawsuit, or even because a lender has refused to renew a sizable note. The strategy behind voluntary bankruptcy in these cases is to get a chance to regroup, to reorganize business finances, and then to take another run at it.

A book that stresses good financial management can't very well *recommend* bankruptcy (which generally occurs due to poor cash management and the resultant inadequacy of working capital). However, we certainly must not ignore the fact that most business ventures go through one or more periods when their cash reserves are dangerously low and when bankruptcy is a distinct possibility. And, even if this kind of crisis never happens to your company, it almost surely will happen to one or more of your customers—and quite possibly you will have had something to do with their bankruptcy. So, you ought to understand what it means to be bankrupt, how a business can get into that condition, and what follows once bankruptcy is declared. In short, the possibility of going bankrupt should be an ingredient of your financial management plan.

Some Legal Aspects of Bankruptcy

The Federal Bankruptcy Act of 1938 provided the foundation for all current legal action. (It has since been amended a number of times, with a major revision taking place in 1973.) It clearly recognizes something which many practicing businessmen have also understood: if a business gets in over its head with debt, something must be done to protect the creditors, but the least desirable action to take is to force the business to suspend operations. If that is done, and if the business assets are then liquidated, everyone is almost sure to lose because second-hand assets never command a respectable price. The proceeds are seldom sufficient to satisfy the claims of all the creditors. Also, as the company is defunct, the principal owner may not be able to reenter the ranks of business leadership.

Involuntary Bankruptcy

The 1938 Bankruptcy Act, as amended, sets up provisions for many "special" kinds of bankruptcy (affecting public utilities, financial institutions, and so on), but two of its chapters pertain to business firms in general. Chapter X governs the form of bankruptcy known as *involuntary,* where the current management of a company is replaced but liquidation is not mandatory (although it does frequently occur). Under this chapter, either the insolvent company itself or three of its creditors whose claims exceed $5,000 in total can petition a bankruptcy court for bankruptcy status.

If the court grants the petition, it then must appoint a trustee who takes over custody of the company. The trustee "safeguards" the company's assets and tries to set up a reorganization plan. At least two-thirds of the creditors and two-thirds of the company ownership must accept the plan. This often fails to happen; also, the trustee may decide that the financial situation is hopeless. In either event, the company's assets must then be disposed of at a bankruptcy sale. All creditors as well as the owner's interest are paid with the money received from the sale according to a preestablished priority of claim.

If one of your customers has ever been involved in an involuntary bankruptcy situation, you know that "general" creditors (such as your company might have been) are next-to-last in the line of those whose claims are paid off. Only the owners have a lower-rated claim; they get what is left after the last debt is settled. The trustee and business appraiser (as well as other court-appointed experts) always receive their fees, but the creditors and the owner are often shortchanged. It's a very unpleasant experience for everyone concerned.

Voluntary Bankruptcy

In contrast, Chapter XI of the Bankruptcy Act provides for a form of bankruptcy that takes less time, involves fewer "experts," and costs much less. This is *voluntary bankruptcy*. Here, the debtor company voluntarily petitions for the status and, if the petition is approved by the court, submits a plan of business reorganization and a procedure for settling the claims of its creditors. After review, and if accepted by the court, a bankruptcy referee then proposes the plan to the "unsecured" creditors, that is, those whose claims are not covered by some kind of collateral. The secured creditors (as well as minority-ownership interests) have no say in considering this reorganization plan, but if it is accepted, they are bound by it. During the bankruptcy proceedings all creditors are legally restrained from harassing the debtor company.

If the reorganization plan is accepted, the principal owner of the debtor company is made personally responsible for implementing it. Once it is completely carried out, the business is declared to be *out of bankruptcy*. During the interim, while the owner is trying to straighten things out, additional money can be borrowed (with any lender getting preference over the older unsecured creditors) and the business can operate in a more or less normal fashion.

Avoiding Involuntary Bankruptcy

It should be mentioned that there are certain illegal acts which always result in *involuntary* bankruptcy and which are definitely to be avoided. These are as follows:

1. *Concealment or fraudulent conveyance of business assets.* Concealment in this case means hiding assets with the intent to defraud creditors. A fraudulent conveyance is the transfer of assets to a third party (rather than to one of the creditors) with the intent to defraud.

2. *Preferential transfer of business assets.* A preferential transfer is a physical transfer of assets or a cash payment to a

preferred creditor, enabling that creditor to receive all of his claim or a larger amount than should be paid to him.

3. *Assignment of business assets.* The assignment of specific property to a creditor in full or partial settlement of his claim is considered to be the equivalent of preferential transfer.

4. *Legal lien on business assets.* If a debtor company permits a creditor to obtain a legal lien on some of the debtor's assets, and then fails to pay or otherwise discharge the lien within 30 days, the debtor company is considered to have granted a preferential transfer. Any other creditor would then be entitled to file a petition for involuntary bankruptcy against the debtor company.

5. *Admission of insolvency in writing.* A *written* admission of insolvency is considered an act of bankruptcy. An insolvent company must therefore be very careful about what the employees put in writing.

Preparing for Voluntary Bankruptcy

Now, let's turn to how you might stay alive even though your business shows every sign of going sour and your creditors are swarming around insistently demanding money. The most important thing you can do is to contact your lawyer—*fast.* (It is assumed that you will have already approached your "friendly" banker and have found him to be suddenly not only unfriendly but decidedly nervous.) If your lawyer feels that voluntary bankruptcy is logical and possible, he will certainly advise you to try to beat your creditors to court, since they may be getting ready to file an involuntary petition. Petitioning for voluntary bankruptcy is not time-consuming, and you won't have to submit your reorganization plan until a reasonable period has passed after the petition is approved.

Incidentally, to be most effective, the plan for reorganizing your business should be very similar to the financial plan for attracting venture capital discussed in Chapter 5. The reason for the similarity is obvious—you will need to convince both the court and your creditors of your ability to make the business profitable again. In addition to the other features of the plan, you must be sure to include one very important item: how you expect to pay off the company's debt. You will want to consider proposing (1) an extension or postponement of payment; (2) substitution of notes for other claims, or the conversion of some of the creditors from an unsecured to a secured status; and (3); reducing the outstanding amount of some claims by issuing corporate stock against a part of the debt.

In the meantime, there are some other secondary actions that must be taken promptly. These actions are as follows:

Your creditors must be appeased. Remember that two-thirds of those unsecured creditors will eventually have to approve your plan for reorganization. They will be skeptical of your intentions and will be well aware that voluntary bankruptcy can easily be used by you as a way to legally "steal" their money. In point of fact, during the voluntary bankruptcy period your creditors will also be among your financiers, since you will be operating to some extent with their money.

Your customers must be reassured. The only chance that the company will have of regaining solvency will be to retain the loyalty of your steady customers. If they continue to do business with you, you may very well be able to make it, but if not you are lost. You will need to contact each of these customers, and explain that their current orders will be filled and that they can count on your company as a future source of supply. The assurance of good continued prospects for customer orders is an absolutely essential element of any reorganization plan.

Your employees must be informed. The hardship due to bankruptcy will probably fall most upon your employees (and your own family). Costs must be cut to the bone, and that usually means wage reductions for all hands, including yourself. You may as well let your personnel know immediately when you file the bankruptcy petition; they are probably as aware of the pressure from creditors as you are. This will be the time to lower fixed costs drastically (which most likely will involve some personnel layoffs), as well as to install stringent cash management if you haven't done it before. All of the tested financial management techniques described in this book will have to be called into play if your company is to regain a healthy operating condition.

The minority owners (if any) must be notified. If anyone else has any equity interest in your business but has no part in the day-to-day operation, that person or persons will be directly affected by a voluntary bankruptcy petition. Their investment is in as much danger as your own, but they will have nothing to say about protective measures. Don't expect such minority owners to be too happy or understanding about the situation, even if they are relatives of yours. But do keep them informed. Remember, if you later need additional equity capital, they may be a source of either more money or recommendations to another lender.

Conclusion

Those who have gone through bankruptcy (the voluntary sort) say that they learned more from it than from any other business experience. Some of the sharpest business managers became that way as the result of a bankruptcy petition. That is why we have treated this subject in a positive way. In reality, bankruptcy is a useful financial management tool in emergencies and should not be dismissed out of hand. *

* It is necessary to enter a disclaimer regarding possible future changes to the present Bankruptcy Act which could invalidate some of the above comments. As we have pointed out, the current legislation actually gives an unscrupulous business owner the license to legally "steal" money from creditors. There are many such abuses taking place these days, and they will not be ignored forever. Also, the bankruptcy court load is often very heavy and time-consuming. Some relief is clearly needed in the form of additional legislation.

12

Managing
Your Business
for a More
Profitable Performance

TO convert financial control techniques into profitable business performance requires effective overall management on your part. This book has presented you with a number of important financial concepts, describing how each can be helpful to your business. But we haven't yet discussed the *coordinated use* of all such management tools. That is what we will take up in this final chapter.

If there is one thing that has not been emphasized enough, it is the need for a comprehensive financial management plan that includes your whole management team. If you intend to install a regular review of your breakeven status, for example, someone will have to do the basic calculations on a routine basis. You may start out by doing the whole thing yourself, but sooner or later you should plan to give the cost- and sales-analysis job to your accountant or bookkeeper. For that matter, the final interpretation of these calculations could be taken over by someone you trust and who would look out for your business interest.

The same approach can be used in projecting a return on your capital investment and in all of the other ways that fiscal data provides vital management information. The first step toward such a subdivision of work is the *assignment*, that is, the delegation of responsibility for the financial data collection and manipulation to one or more specific employees. The second step is *integration*—meshing the performance of the financial functions with all of the other routine business operations that your employees perform. That last step is *economy*, meaning, getting the job done as efficiently as possible so that you are presented with timely and accurate reports, useful for planning and directing the company operations.

Don't assume that the last two steps will happen of their own accord, without any direction on your part. You need a plan of attack to install comprehensive financial management, just as much as you need a plan to carry out any of the other important activities performed by your company.

What to Expect from Your Accountant or Bookkeeper

If you use your accountant or bookkeeper properly, that is, if you guide and direct him or her toward accomplishing what you want, then your comprehensive financial management program will be under way. Without any direction from you, the accounting system of your company will be mainly a method of recording, collecting, and reporting fiscal data. But under your direction, another function can be added— that of *analyzing*, summarizing and comparing the information reported and then supplying the proper person with the results of that analysis. There are universal accounting rules and procedures which must be followed for your business when determining profit for tax purposes, for example, or when financial statements are prepared for presentation to a bank. However, above and beyond these standard requirements, you can have a virtually free hand in tailoring the variety and format of the data to be brought together for your review.

Your Own Participation—and That of Your Key Subordinates

It goes without saying that the financial accomplishments of any type of business will be due to administrative talent as well as to the compilation of data. Entries on a sheet of paper will certainly be useful in various ways, but by themselves the figures contribute nothing. They aren't able to discuss or interpret; they can't talk back.

From the viewpoint of your business, a complete and timely report on some phase of activity can be worth a great deal or very little, depending upon what is done as the result of it. If you neglect to take action, or if the action is delayed too long, all of the work required to compile that report will be wasted. But if the analysis is promptly reviewed and then used as the basis for corrective steps, or as a guide for future direction and control, then the compilation of figures can be a vital management tool. In either case, the only variable or unknown factor will be the ultimate applicability of the analysis. Regardless of the principles of financial management by exception, you cannot always expect to carry out every study or make each decision for the company by yourself. You should no doubt, play a major role, but in certain situations you will need assistance.

To some extent the kind of help you can get will depend on the size of the company. If your company is very small, you have probably been making and will continue to make most of the important decisions alone. If yours is a larger business, there are likely to be one or two other key people with whom you share the load. A question you should think about is how *structured* should the financial decision making be for your business, and how solidly should the direction and control be organized to carry out those decisions?

What we are leading up to is the need for a financial management plan. The foundation of the plan will have to be provided by you, and will depend on how you want the business to operate, the priorities you set, the strategies you want to follow. However, once you complete that first step, financial goals and targets can be established and the level of necessary financial resources or limits can be set in a manner quite similar to the advance planning discussed in Chapter 2 relating to developing a cash budget. Then you will have the means for some decision-making assignments; then you can make someone else responsible for at least part of the financial management of your company.

Of course, to implement such a program, you will have to delegate some authority to one or more subordinates. But a word of caution: if you decide to do this, be sure to provide sharply focused assignments. That's the only way to ensure that your exact intentions are carried out. It can create serious problems if you think that you were assigning certain financial tasks only to find out later that they were not really being performed the way you wanted.

So, what would justify converting to such a financial management "work plan"? Why should you consider giving away some of your financial authority? For only one reason—the potential for greater profitability. If other key people in your organization begin to understand your financial facts of life the business can only benefit. The term "knowledge worker" has been coined to describe the people in an organization who really make it function. The more knowledge workers there are, the more effectively the business can operate. If you adopt this approach, your job will not be any less important. You will still be the final authority, just as though you had kept all the financial decision making for yourself. You will simply direct and motivate the key staff to accomplish what you want.

Conclusion

If you are the typical small-business owner, you probably devote much more time and thought to conducting your business affairs than to your private life. The purpose of this book has been to try to simplify the fiscal side of your business by explaining some effective techniques for financial management, and thus to help cut down on your work time.

There is no real training or break-in period for managing a business financially. You simply must learn by doing it, and mistakes are often expensive in the most painful sort of way—the cost comes out of your own pocket. But by using this text as a how-to guide, it is hoped that you will avoid some of the possible errors and eliminate many of your worries. No small-business owner can ever know enough to absolutely ensure profitable operation; however, it is possible to become better and better at managing and in that way to improve the odds for success. If this book helps you toward that end, it will have accomplished its purpose.

APPENDIX

"To Whom It May Concern"— Two Mathematical Derivations

IF you are the sort of reader who wants proof of some of the mathematics contained in the text, this appendix has been included especially for you.

Derivation of the Breakeven Point of Sales Formula

The way to prove the validity of this formula is to manipulate the basic figures in another way. Let's start with the calculation performed for ABC Toolcraft, contained in Chapter 7.

$$\text{Breakeven Point of Sales} = \frac{\$36,330}{100\% - 52.5\%}$$

$$= \frac{\$36,330}{47.5\%} \text{ or } \frac{\$36,330}{.475}$$

Proof

Amount of Sales at Breakeven Point.................	= $76,484
(minus) Variable Cost at Breakeven (52.5% of sales) .	−40,154
Gross Margin.....................................	= $36,330
(minus) Fixed Cost...............................	−36,330
Net Profit	= $00,000

Calculation of the Present Value of $1 (Table 5)

To prove the entire table is an unnecessary exercise, since every value is calculated by the same formula. Therefore, we will simply derive the present value of $1 discounted at 4 percent and to be received two years hence. The table shows this amount to be 0.925.

Proof

The present value of $1 to be received n years from today, at a discount rate r, is determined by the following algebraic formula:

$$\frac{1}{(1 + r)^n}$$

Therefore, the present value of $1 to be received two years from now at a 4 percent discount rate is calculated as follows:

$$\text{Present Value} = \frac{1}{(1 + .04)^n} = \frac{1}{(1.04)^2} = \frac{1}{1.0816}$$

$$= .9245562 = .925 \text{ (rounded)}$$

Recommended Readings

Bittel, Lester R. *Management by Exception*. New York: McGraw-Hill, 1964.

Cohn, Theodore, and Roy A. Lindberg. *Survival and Growth: Management Strategies for the Small Firm*. New York: AMACOM, 1974.

✓Dible, Donald M. *Up Your Own Organization*. Santa Clara, Calif.: The Entrepreneur Press, 1974.

✓Drucker, Peter F. *Managing for Results*. New York: Harper & Row, 1964.

Jones, Reginald L., and H. George Trenton. *Budgeting: Key to Planning and Control*. New York: AMACOM, 1971.

Lamb, Tony, and Dave Duffy. *The Retirement Threat*. Los Angeles: J. P. Tarcher, 1977 (distributed by St. Martin's Press, New York).

Index

AMACOM Executive Books—Paperbacks

John Applegath	Working Free	$6.95
John D. Arnold	The Art of Decision Making: 7 Steps to Achieving More Effective Results	$6.95
Alec Benn	The 27 Most Common Mistakes in Advertising	$5.95
Dudley Bennett	TA and the Manager	$6.95
Don Berliner	Want a Job? Get Some Experience ...	$5.95
Blake & Mouton	Productivity—The Human Side	$5.95
Borst & Montana	Managing Nonprofit Organizations	$6.95
George A. Brakeley	Tested Ways to Successful Fund Raising	$8.95
Ronald D. Brown	From Selling to Managing	$5.95
Richard E. Byrd	A Guide to Personal Risk Taking	$5.95
Logan Cheek	Zero-Base Budgeting Comes of Age	$6.95
William A. Cohen	The Executive's Guide to Finding a Superior Job	$5.95
Ken Cooper	Bodybusiness	$5.95
James J. Cribbin	Effective Managerial Leadership	$6.95
William Dowling	Effective Management & the Behavioral Sciences	$8.95
Richard J. Dunsing	You and I Have Simply Got to Stop Meeting This Way	$5.95
Sidney Edlung	There *Is* a Better Way to Sell	$5.95
Elam & Paley	Marketing for the Nonmarketing Executive	$5.95
Norman L. Enger	Management Standards for Developing Information Systems	$6.95
John Fenton	The A to Z of Sales Management	$7.95
Figueroa & Winkler	A Business Information Guidebook	$9.95
Saul W. Gellerman	Motivation and Productivity	$6.95
Roger A. Golde	Muddling Through	$5.95
Hanan Berrian, Cribbin, & Donis	Success Strategies for the New Sales Manager	$8.95
Lois B. Hart	Moving Up! Women and Leadership	$6.95
Hart & Schleicher	A Conference and Workshop Planner's Manual	$15.95
Michael Hayes	Pay Yourself First	$6.95
Hilton & Knoblauch	On Television	$6.95
Herman R. Holtz	The $100 Billion Market	$10.95
Herman R. Holtz	Profit From Your Money-Making Ideas	$8.95
Charles L. Hughes	Goal Setting	$5.95
John W. Humble	How to Manage By Objectives	$5.95
Jones & Trentin	Budgeting (rev. ed.)	$12.95
Donald J. Kenney	Minicomputers	$7.95
William H. Krause	How to Get Started as a Manufacturers' Representative	$8.95
Sy Lazarus	Loud & Clear: A Guide to Effective Communication	$5.95